WHEN FRIENDSHIP FEELS HARD

God's design for *deep* relationships

AMBER ALBEE SWENSON

Published by Straight Talk Books
P.O. Box 301, Milwaukee, WI 53201
800.661.3311 · timeofgrace.org

Printed in the United States of America

ISBN: 978-1-965694-42-8

Contents

Introduction

My husband, Steve, and I arrived at the airport at 1:00 P.M. Our flight, which was scheduled to leave at 4:00, had already been delayed. Shortly after we were supposed to board, an announcement was made that mechanical issues would have us grounded until at least 6:00. The next announcement said the plane wasn't usable.

By this time, Steve was talking with the third of our children to check in on us. One had FaceTimed us on her way home from school. (Don't worry; she wasn't driving.) The second had called after he got home from work. And the third had just called when I looked up and saw the familiar faces of friends I stay with sometimes when I go to Appleton, Wisconsin. (We have a fourth child, but she had been the one to bring us coffee when she and our daughter-in-law dropped us off at the airport.)

I hurried over to greet my friends. They were in the process of getting on a different flight, and in a few minutes, Steve and I were booked on that flight too. The airline gave us vouchers to eat, so we enjoyed a meal together and then walked to our gate. They are two rows in front of us right now. And somewhere along the line when I wondered out loud if our luggage made it from one plane to the next (it did), we decided that even if it didn't, it was probably worth it to have started our adventure before our adventure . . . together.

Relationships are important. I often wear three bracelets to remind me just how important they are. One bracelet reads, "Made to worship." It was given to me by my oldest daughter, and it represents my relationship with God. He is worthy of my worship whether the plane is delayed or on time, whether I feel good or have a migraine, whether he decides to answer my prayers the way I hoped or not.

The second bracelet is braided yarn made by and gifted to me several years ago by my youngest daughter. It represents family. After my relationship with God, my family members are the ones I do life with most.

The third bracelet was given to me at a women's retreat by a woman I sat across from at lunch. After I got done speaking, she handed me the bracelet. It reminds me of the amazing people I often meet and the many people I've never met but who are on the other side of a screen or a book or in a pew or a chair whom I get the privilege of ministering to. I don't know their stories or the particulars of their lives. Many of them I would befriend if time and circumstance allowed.

A few months ago, I was at a leadership conference. Two of my closest friends were also attending the conference, and we decided to have supper together. Another friend joined us.

At some point in the meal, we started talking about eternity. In the Bible when Jesus went up a mountain with his disciples Peter, James, and John and showed his glory to them, the prophets Moses and Elijah appeared there with them. Peter, James, and John knew exactly who Moses and Elijah were by sight, even though they had not met them. God permitted them to recognize Moses and Elijah. I'm not sure how it will work once we're living in eternity, but I think it's likely we will just know who people are too.

One of my friends who is both whimsical and wise loves to skip. I told her I would see her from afar and know her when I saw her skipping.

I turned to the next friend. She would be surrounded by dogs.

The newer friend who had joined us for dinner is a connoisseur of wine. I would know her by the glass of wine in her hand.

Then one of my friends asked, "Amber, how will we know you?"

"I will be the one surrounded by friends," I said.

I consider my godly friends—the people I walk and pray with, read the Bible with, meet for lunch or coffee—to be one of God's greatest treasures. If you find people who like to be around you; whom you like to be around; whom you can be yourself with and feel connected to; who will encourage you, pray for you, admonish and hold you accountable, well, you are wealthier than most.

God, family, friends, others. That is the relationship recipe that adds layers of fulfillment to our existence.

—Amber

Chapter 1

God Loves Community

The first three verses of the Bible introduce us to the concept of community:

> **In the beginning God created the heavens and the earth. Now the earth was formless and empty, darkness was over the surface of the deep, and the Spirit of God was hovering over the waters.**
>
> **And God said, "Let there be light," and there was light.** (Genesis 1:1–3)

Verse 1 introduces us to God the Father, but already in verse 2, we find out God the Father was not alone. The Spirit of God, sometimes referred to as the Holy Spirit, was there too.

We might miss the second person of the Trinity at creation—who appears throughout the Old Testament as the Angel of the Lord and came to earth in human form as Jesus—if it wasn't for Jesus' disciple and good friend John who wrote:

In the beginning was the Word, and the Word was with God, and the Word was God. He was with God in the beginning. Through him all things were made; without him nothing was made that has been made. The Word became flesh and made his dwelling among us. We have seen his glory, the glory of the one and only Son, who came from the Father, full of grace and truth. For the law was given through Moses; grace and truth came through Jesus Christ. (John 1:1–3,14,17)

John tells us Jesus was present at creation. All three persons—God the Father, God the Son, and God the Holy Spirit—appeared as one God, coexisting in community.*

The word *community* has its origin in the word *communis*, which means "common, shared by all or many." According to Google, the word encapsulates the idea of "sharedness" (which is now my new favorite word). It's about coming together and sharing experiences, interests, spaces, and common goals.

The Father, Son, and Holy Spirit always have and always will embody community in its purest form. They exist in

---

* If the idea of the Trinity is new to you, here's a quick lesson: God the Father is often referred to as the first person in the Trinity; Jesus, or God's Son, is the second person of the Trinity, and the Holy Spirit is the third person of the Trinity. They aren't three gods. They are one God with three distinct identities. They are all equal. They have different roles but work in conjunction with the other two persons.

complete sharedness. Their interests and goals are not just common; they are identical. What the Father wants, the Son wants, and the Spirit wants. Here's proof:

Jesus started his public ministry on the banks of the Jordan River when he was baptized by a man called John the Baptist. The apostle Matthew records that John was born to prepare the world for Jesus. He did that by pointing out people's shortcomings. Once a person's heart was open and they recognized their sin and had a desire to change, John baptized them into a new life as a child of God. He taught the people how to leave their former lives and live differently, not as greedy extortionists or power-hungry thugs but as God-fearing and loving men and women who cared about others.

John the Baptist knew Jesus was the Son of God and the long-awaited Messiah. When Jesus came to him to be baptized, John didn't think it would be right for him, a flawed man, to baptize the perfect Son of God. And yet Jesus insisted on being baptized. My *Concordia Self-Study Bible* gives four reasons why.

1. It marked the beginning of Jesus' ministry and him being set apart for God's purposes.
2. It gave John an occasion to announce publicly that Jesus was the Messiah.
3. Jesus, though sinless, identified with our sin and failures in Baptism. He would become sin for us as our substitute.
4. It served as an example to his followers.[1]

When Jesus came out of the river after his baptism, we see the unity of sharedness of the Father, Son, and Spirit. Just as they were unified in mission at the creation of the world, the Father, Son, and Spirit were unified in mission at Jesus' baptism. The Spirit descended on Jesus in the form of a dove and expressed his approval silently. The Father expressed his approval openly, saying, **"This is my Son, whom I love; with him I am well pleased"** (Matthew 3:17).

Father, Son, and Spirit were one in mission. They totally agreed on the work Jesus was about to do to win our salvation. The religious people of Jesus' day had muddied God's law and plan of rescue. They preached that heaven and a right relationship with God were attainable by working hard. They made the law complicated and heavy. The Father and Spirit showed their support and sharedness in the work the Son was doing to take the burden of a right relationship with God off of people, which was unattainable, and to put that burden on Jesus, who could and would make it happen.

Throughout his ministry, Jesus showed alignment with the Father and the Spirit. One time, the Spirit led Jesus into the wilderness to be tempted. Jesus followed because it was his Father's will that he did so.

Jesus often referred to "my time." The note in my study Bible explains: "Jesus moved in accordance with the will of God."[2] That is to say, Jesus wasn't acting on his own, doing whatever he wanted to do whenever he wanted to do it. His sense of timing was in line with the will of God.

In John 4:4 it says that Jesus **"*had* to go through**

Samaria." Why did he have to go there? Again, my study Bible explains: "The necessity lay in Jesus' mission, not in geography."[3] Whether it was aligning himself to the Father's timetable or the Father's mission, Jesus resolutely acted in accordance with the will and plan of the Father. He went where the Father wanted him to go and did what the Father wanted him to do when the Father wanted him to do it.

Jesus openly told the religious leaders of his time, the Pharisees, **"Very truly I tell you, the Son can do nothing by himself; he can do only what he sees his Father doing, because whatever the Father does the Son also does"** (John 5:19).

Jesus wasn't looking for anyone's approval, and he wasn't doing miracles to win crowds or status. He was aligned to the Father's agenda and timetable for his life and ministry. The sharedness of the Trinity required him to submit to the plan.

The community of the Trinity is an example for us. That sense of sharing in mission, love, and experiences is what motivates us to do life with others who share our beliefs. If there's a section of Scripture that gives us a goal to aim for, it is Acts 2:44–47:

> **All the believers were together and had everything in common. They sold property and possessions to give to anyone who had need. Every day they continued to meet together in the temple courts. They broke bread in their homes and ate together with**

glad and sincere hearts, praising God and enjoying the favor of all the people. And the Lord added to their number daily those who were being saved.

Note that first sentence. The believers had everything in common. Their mission was to walk with God and to serve his people while telling anyone who would listen about God's goodness as seen in the life and work of Jesus Christ. They ate together, praised God together, shared with each other.

Togetherness is good, great even, and it's a powerful witness to the unbelieving world. While the world was busy chasing after stuff, these believers were happy selling their stuff. While the world gave into the doldrums, these believers met with glad and sincere hearts.

From the very beginning of created time, God determined being alone was not a desired outcome. Every day as God created, he looked at what he had done and said the same thing: It was good.

"God saw that the light was good" (Genesis 1:4).

When he looked at the sky and the seas, **"God saw that it was good"** (Genesis 1:10).

When he looked at the trees and vegetation, **"God saw that it was good"** (Genesis 1:12).

When he looked at the sun, moon, stars, and planets, **"God saw that it was good"** (Genesis 1:18).

When he saw the fish and the birds and all the living creatures, **"God saw that it was good"** (Genesis 1:25).

Then we're told:

> **Now the LORD God had formed out of the ground all the wild animals and all the birds in the sky. He brought them to the man to see what he would name them; and whatever the man called each living creature, that was its name. So the man gave names to all the livestock, the birds in the sky and all the wild animals.**
>
> **But for Adam no suitable helper was found.** (Genesis 2:19,20)

Every day as God looked at what he had done, it was good. But when God looked at Adam, he could not say it was good. In fact, he said: **"It is *not good* for the man to be alone. I will make a helper suitable for him"** (Genesis 2:18, emphasis mine). After Adam had a suitable helper in Eve, then God saw that it was **"very good"** (Genesis 1:31).

That's not to say that every person needs to be married in order to live a full life. Some of my favorite people in the world have never been married and live very full lives, lives that others envy. But they don't live their lives alone. In fact, the single people I know who thrive are rarely alone. Their schedules are such that I rally for a chance to see them.

A study published in October 2024 found a key component to satisfaction among young singles. Do you want to guess what it was?

> One of the standout findings from our study is

> how deeply friendships shape happiness for single emerging adults. We found that singles who were satisfied with their friendships tended to be happy with their lives, while those dissatisfied with their friendships were less happy. In short, the quality of your friendships is a key factor for your well-being, especially if you're single.[4]

I've found the same to be true of almost every age group. The people I know who are the most joy filled, least irritable, most grateful, and most content are the people who have and continue to develop deep and meaningful relationships. Some people have one or two good friends, and as long as they have those people, they have all they need. Their roots go deep. They like to enjoy and appreciate everything together. Quantity isn't as important as quality.

Others make friends easily and prefer to hang out with all kinds of people. Those people find friends wherever they are. Put them on a bus, on a cruise ship, in an airplane, and before they get off, they will be talking about their greatest joys, biggest regrets, the meaning of life, and the best coffee they've ever had.

When I worked in a nursing home, I saw both extremes. There were residents who kept to themselves and didn't let anyone in. And there were residents who would talk to anyone and everyone. There was a group of men who had very different life experiences but who bonded at the table they sat at every meal. Once in a while they talked about baseball or the weather, but mostly they talked about their decision to eat smaller portions because by and large they were served far too much food. Other than that, the only words spoken were a greeting when they arrived to eat and a goodbye when they left.

Recently, when I went back to the nursing home nearly two years after I last worked there, I talked to and had a beautiful conversation and laughs with two sweet women whom I always enjoyed caring for. One rarely leaves her room except on bath day. The other rarely stays in her room unless she isn't feeling well. I'm positive neither remembered me, and I had incredible, memorable interactions with both, in part because they were both open to it. Both have dementia, so good relationships aren't bound entirely by mental capacity as much as being open to relationship and conversation.

Elijah was God's Old Testament prophet during the reign of wicked King Ahab and Queen Jezebel. They introduced Baal worship to Israel, and Elijah preached against it. Doing so made him a stench to Ahab and Jezebel and finally put him on their most wanted list. After a particularly tense standoff, Elijah escaped to the desert, fleeing for his life.

Circumstances being what they were, Elijah didn't have a cell phone to call a friend to pick him up physically, mentally, or spiritually. He was all alone, worn out, without a plan. In fact, the only plan he could imagine as an effective solution to his predicament was to die. First Kings chapter 19 tells us:

He came to a broom bush, sat down under it and prayed that he might die. "I have had enough, Lord," he said. "Take my life; I am no better than my ancestors." Then he lay down under the bush and fell asleep.

All at once an angel touched him and said, "Get up and eat." He looked around, and there by his head was some bread baked over hot coals, and a jar of water. He ate and drank and then lay down again.

The angel of the Lord came back a second time and touched him and said, "Get up and eat, for the journey is too much for you." So he got up and ate and drank. Strengthened by that food, he traveled forty days and forty nights until he reached Horeb, the mountain of God. (verses 4–8)

I don't know if you've ever been where Elijah was: overwhelmed and understaffed. He had been through three and a half years living with a widow and her son and staying out of sight because Ahab wanted to kill him. He finally appeared before Ahab, had a massive confrontation, and then ran for his life.

When he was alone, he wanted to die. I could guess Elijah had reasons for running to the desert. Maybe he didn't want to implicate anyone else in the manhunt Ahab and Jezebel had for him. Maybe he thought he'd be better off alone.

When we're all alone, trying to deal with overwhelming stress, it's easy to sink into despair. When Elijah prayed, God didn't allow Elijah to be alone for long. When no one else was around to comfort Elijah, God himself ("the angel of the LORD") made him food and gave him water to drink.

There are times in your life when you are uncomfortably alone. When my husband had hip surgery earlier this year, I could only stay with him for a bit. When he went into the operating room, he had to go alone. He was alone in the recovery room until they brought him to his post-op room.

If you live long enough, your spouse and most of your friends may die before you. Most of us will face death alone. Even if the room is full of people we love, we are the only ones who slip from this world into eternity at that time.

And yet as we see with Elijah and as Jesus himself promised, he will see to it that we are never alone. Jesus told his disciples and us, **"Surely I am with you always, to the very end of the age"** (Matthew 28:20).

Throughout the Bible, we see God with his people. When Jesus took on flesh and blood, the name God gave him was Immanuel, which means "God with us."

All this is to say that relationships matter to God, and they should matter to us. If you've struggled to find people to walk with you through life, let's explore roadblocks and look at things that may help.

Don't worry about diving into the deep end right away. As you ponder this chapter, just dip a toe into the water with small first steps you can do to have better relationships.

Dip a toe in:

1. God loves community. If you are lonely, pray for friends. God hears.

2. Read Psalm 25. David, an Old Testament king of God's people who went through many struggles in his life, admitted he was lonely. What reminders did he give himself? What did he pray for?

3. How might this lead you to pray?

4. Which relationships do you long for most?

Chapter 2

The Things That Keep Us From the Relationships We Long to Have

No one, and I mean no one, wants to think they may be sabotaging themselves. All of us would rather point a finger somewhere else, anywhere else, to keep the blame from landing near us. That's not helpful. One of Jesus' most famous quotes says:

> **"Why do you look at the speck of sawdust in your brother's eye and pay no attention to the plank in your own eye? How can you say to your brother, 'Let me take the speck out of your eye,' when all the time there is a plank in your own eye? You hypocrite, first take the plank out of your own eye, and then you will see clearly to remove the speck from your brother's eye."** (Matthew 7:3–5)

Jesus' point is that we almost always recognize what someone else is doing to sabotage their journey, but rarely, if ever, are we self-aware enough to realize we are doing things that sabotage us. In this chapter, I'm going to address three common things that might be keeping you from good friendships. And because it's one thing to know but another thing to do something about it, after each problem area, I'll give some helpful hints to help you change.

But first I want to assure you that no one does this perfectly. In this broken world, we all mess up. So as you read, learn from these mistakes, know you are forgiven in Jesus, and pray for God's wisdom as you have conversations with others, showing Jesus' love as you do it.

If as you read this chapter you start to feel down about past mistakes, please remember God's grace and move forward in it.

1. Not knowing how to talk to others keeps people from good relationships.

I see this over and over. I wish the art of conversation was taught in school. Let me explain.

A conversation by definition is a talk between two or more people in which news and ideas are discussed and explained. Here's how so many of us get this wrong.

We share too much. Exchanging information should be just that—both people talking. When one person dominates the conversation, that exchange is stifled. All too often we engage in verbal vomiting. We call someone or walk to their office or sit down next to them and tell them everything that hasn't gone according to plan in the last 2, 3, 6, 24, or 48 hours. Unless there's good reason, no one needs to know that your cat threw up or you didn't get the parking spot or that you went to put milk in your coffee and forgot you used the last of it the day before. It's not just you. And as those things happen, we clean up the puke, drive on, and make a mental note to pick milk up on the way home, while hopefully thanking God for the cat, the car, and the coffee that's delicious whether we have milk or not.

So if the vast majority of your conversation is a litany of complaints, it's hard to listen to. If you're generally a joyful person and once in a while report you are having a bad day, no problem. If something unusually bad happens, others want to hear about it. And if everything has gone wrong consistently since the moment you got out of bed, like in the book *Alexander and the Terrible, Horrible, No Good, Very Bad Day*, that's altogether different. Let someone know so they can pray for you and, depending on severity, laugh with you.

Tell someone when you stand in front of a coffee pot for a ridiculous amount of time before realizing it was unplugged. Let them know when you leave your office and walk all over the building looking for your sweater, only to return to your office to find your sweater on the back of your chair. Other people can relate, and it helps them feel better about their own lives when they hear someone else does the same things they do. By all means, if you're in the middle of an ordeal, whether it's a sick child or a parent in a nursing home or a parent who should be in a nursing home but isn't, other people get it. Your friends want to hear about those things. But the key here is frequency.

It's hard to befriend someone who consistently reports every bad thing. If every day is terrible and every week is worse than the last, you could benefit from considering different life choices to bring you to different places and bringing gratitude into your days. Remember, Jesus loves you. As you work to be more grateful and sometimes fall short, he is there to help you.

Your brain looks for whatever you tell it to focus on. If you focus on the bad, it will find it. If, however, you take note of the kind email, the sunshine, and the neighbor who waved, your brain starts to notice other things that give you a reason to pause and think life isn't so bad. Your glasses help you see; your shoes make walking so much easier than it would be otherwise. You have a roof over your head and a bed to sleep in. There are leaves on the trees and blooming flowers . . . so many things. It's always refreshing to hear someone point out these things.

We overwhelm others with details. When you're explaining what happened to your mother's second cousin on the paternal side, unless your listener can somehow relate or it's relevant to a point you are trying to make, most people will struggle to keep up. In today's world, we've got information coming at us all day every day, so it's important to sift information into what is relevant and what is nonessential.

Unless a person asks for every detail, details should be limited to what moves a conversation forward. The goal is neither to hide details nor to overwhelm a person with details. If most of the conversation can be summed up in a few words, do it. If the other person wants to know more, they are likely to ask for more.

We're afraid of silence. A blog post titled, "The Role of Silence in Conversation" advises silence is important to genuine conversation, especially in the workplace. It allows the other person to gather their thoughts rather than blurt out the first thing that comes to mind. Introverts especially require a little more time to get comfortable speaking. Giving them silence tells them you are willing to wait for their good ideas.[5] Years ago, a friend taught me that extroverts talk to think but introverts think to talk. Don't worry if 30 seconds pass. Wait for them to say something, and if they don't, maybe the conversation is over.

We're not truthful. "You're the best!" "You look so good!" "I'm sure it was the other person's fault!" While it's nice to hear compliments, the compliments need to be honest and measured. No one is great all the time or looks great all the time or is always right. Give compliments when you are sincere about the compliments, but also give warnings and rebuke when needed. I depend on my friends' honesty. I look to my friends to hold me accountable and point out to me the things I miss, even if what I'm missing is something I need to change. Don't try to be the nicest person in the room if it is misleading.

We are so consumed with wanting to be heard that we put out a vibe that we genuinely don't care about the other person. My children have quit talking to a certain relative who spends every gathering reporting every minute detail of their life while never asking anything about theirs. It's sad to think of the relationships this person has missed out on because they refuse to be invested even a little in the life of someone else.

We don't let anyone in. Every time someone asks, we are fine, good, everything is great. I don't know anyone who is good all the time. Covering up and refusing to talk about the struggles we have keeps everyone at arm's length. It doesn't allow our friends to comfort, support, or encourage us. And while you don't want to report every detail to every person, it's usually comforting when a person admits something they struggle with.

Conversation doesn't have to be difficult. Genuinely ask people about their lives. Don't be overly concerned about telling them about yours. If you've been speaking for a while, ask them a question. Talk about ideas rather than people and real life rather than news, unless the news is worthy of being talked about because the storm is bigger than most or the tragedy is extreme.

When you read the gospels, you never find Jesus complaining. Even when people were trying to trick him, Jesus cut to the heart of the matter and avoided the controversial ditches people were hoping he'd jump in. He never sinned. He knew the truth of situations. He could have spent his time correcting everyone about everything. But he didn't, except in the case of the religious leaders who were leading people astray.

Even so, Jesus didn't shy away from tough conversations. He met with a Samaritan woman at a well and pointed out her sin. He met with a church leader named Nicodemus who didn't understand the basics of his relationship with God.

So, too, when we are sincere and when we don't shy away from tough subjects, even ones that implicate us because of something we've done in our past or we're still dealing with even now, people learn to trust us. No one has all the answers, and no one expects you to. Honesty, sincerity, and vulnerability will take you pretty far when it comes to good conversation.

2. Sin keeps people from relationships.

Do people tend to shy away from you or not invite you to things and you don't have a clue why? You sense an absence of close connection but have never considered there are things you do to drive people away—things that are not God-pleasing. If so, it's time for self-examination.

Do you gossip? Have people quit talking to you because they're pretty sure whatever they say will go right to the next person?

Do you lie or exaggerate? Have your stories caught up with you and people don't invite you anymore because they know you make things up?

Are you a manipulator or controller? Nothing is ever your fault. Everyone else is to blame, and no one does anything as well as you do.

Do you glory in the wickedness of the world? The stories and jokes you tell are not the stories a godly person would tell at the table. When you recount the wild days of youth with pleasure, might you be offending those you're telling?

You've no doubt heard this saying: Show me your friends, and I'll show you your future. Right now, that may be daunting.

Know this. You can repent, turn, change, and start over. God is merciful. He meets you and me with grace. Every time we're ready to start over, he will cheer us on and give us the strength to do so. After King David in the Bible committed adultery with a woman named Bathsheba and had her husband killed, he penned Psalm 51. He said, **"A broken and contrite heart you, God, will not despise"** (verse 17).

That's so good to know. God doesn't hate us when we come to him acknowledging we've blown it. And there's a good chance those around us will applaud our sincere desire to do life differently too. You may be surprised at how eager your friends are to help you when you are ready to change.

Take an honest look at your life. When you long to be different, to make different choices, and to be around people who hold you to a higher standard and see potential in you that you don't see in yourself, what can you do to change? Make one different choice; take one small step. Even the smallest choices, made consistently, can make a big difference.

If you've struggled with gossiping, determine to stop. Every time you go to say something, ask yourself: "Do I need to say this? Is this my news to tell?" If the gossip flows freely when you go to coffee with a certain person, stop going to coffee, or ask that person to stop you if you start saying something you shouldn't.

If you've struggled to control everything, including the narrative you tell everyone else, the first step is realizing this is a form of manipulation. You are not perfect. And your family isn't always the problem. Sometimes your actions caused the tense evening you had. Sometimes your attitude hurts the feelings of those closest to you. Admit it instead of making excuses so the people around you can encourage you as you make different choices.

I struggled with control when my oldest started driving. It took me a bit, but I slowly realized I needed to let go. I needed to put her safety in God's hands so I didn't drive her crazy and put an irreparable wedge between us. My older friends who had already been through it were instrumental in helping me understand. They reminded me that we didn't have phones when we started driving. I drove all the way to Chicago when I was 18, and my parents didn't know anything about my whereabouts until I returned four days later.

When we let our friends in and give them permission to speak truthfully to us, they can tell us when we're being unreasonable and hold us to a higher standard.

The problem, of course, is that we don't see our own weaknesses or take responsibility for what *we* do. We can always see *their* weaknesses. But when it comes to our own, we are often clueless.

Can you find a solution to whatever your struggle is? Now more than ever, we have access to experts. Making changes is often a matter of making informed choices. When you know better, you do better. Sounds easy, right? A lot of times it isn't.

A lot of times we're so overwhelmed with life that any change, no matter how small, seems overwhelming. That's why it's important to make small changes and commit to them completely.

If you are able, identify your weaknesses; identify a solution; ask God to help and guide you; and take small, easy, and consistent steps. One step after another in the right direction, over time, takes you to a completely different place. And if you aren't able, consider asking a mature Christian to help you identify what you can't.

Don't forget to celebrate your wins. I tend to go right from one goal to the next without taking the time to stop and thank God for progress made. That's a mistake. And then, when your life and habits are a little more under control, you can be an encouragement to others and so much better at relationships. Previously, I mentioned the table of men in the dining room at the nursing home where I worked. The four men changed from time to time as people died, but when one chair was vacated, another male resident was put at the table. And during the time I was there, those men consistently asked for smaller servings. They refused to overeat and mentioned often that there was just way too much food. Those men made choices to restrict their caloric intake and spurred one another on to do the same. They encouraged each other as friends do! They could have eaten everything and asked for more. Instead, they reminded each other that if they wanted to keep walking and moving, they needed to keep their weight down.

3. A sour, critical attitude (think Ebenezer Scrooge or the Grinch), repels good relationships in the same way Scrooge and the Grinch did.

One of my first jobs was in a bakery. The head baker did not like me or mornings or smiles. Every morning I greeted her with, "Good morning!" Every morning she grunted. She scowled and answered my questions with snide comments and a petty tone. When I asked other people why she was always in such a bad mood, they said she had a tough life.

I'm not sure if she had a tough life because of her bad attitude or if she had a bad attitude because of her tough life. Whatever you are going through will still be the same whether or not you let people in, find things to be grateful for, and treat people with kindness and respect. So I encourage you to let people in, find things to be grateful for, and treat the people around you with kindness and respect.

The last time our family went to the Boundary Waters, we knew my husband wouldn't be able to carry much on the portage (trails) because he had hip surgery a few months prior.* We didn't expect one of my daughters to get sick

* The Boundary Waters are a series of lakes between Minnesota and Canada. You can hike, fish, and camp there, but you have to carry everything in and out again. The paths between lakes are called portages. Some portages are steep and rocky. There are roots and branches to avoid while carrying your packs and/or canoe.

either. When she did, we were down two people, which meant the rest of us had to do even more work.

We started our last morning with prayer. Our steepest portage was just ahead. We'd have to climb 150 feet carrying our heavy bags and three canoes up a series of rock steps that aren't easy to climb without anything on our backs or shoulders. And we'd each have to do it three times. So as I prayed, I asked God for strength while thanking him for the beautiful day, for legs and arms that worked, and for the opportunity to praise him as we went about our day.

When I finished, my son said, "Mom, you are the only one who would pray that way."

I told him: "The portages will be the same no matter what. We can grumble our way through, or we can thank the Lord and ask him for strength."

And that's true in life. If every time someone asks, we tell them it's a bad day and a horrible week and everyone else is the reason why, chances are our attitudes are the problem. Because, yes, things happen consistently, but those are just the normal annoyances of life in a sinful world. Those are not meant to bring us down or give us reason to grumble. Those minor irritations that happen to everyone every day are the constant reminders that we aren't home yet. This world isn't perfect, and heaven will be so much better.

If you do have good reason to complain because the job or the house or the yard or whatever really is too much, do your best to change whatever the situation is that makes you hate the situation you are in. For example, if you aren't able to make ten thousand dollars less a year to get a different job so you love what you do, then strive to honor God right where you are until something changes. If you can't get a new job, praise God at this job while looking and praying for another. If you think that's impossible because your job really is the absolute worst, look at the examples from the Bible of Joseph in the book of Genesis or Daniel and his friends in the book of Daniel. None of them picked where they were or what they did. And yet, they served with excellence, even in conditions that were less than ideal.

Or if your yard is a constant thorn in your side and you can't move or get rid of all your flower beds or hire someone to do the work, can you get rid of one flower bed? Consider asking friends if they'd like your perennials, and invite them over to dig what they want. Or put the plants on Facebook Marketplace for free, or dig them up and put them on the curb with a note that anyone who wants them can have them to enjoy.

If all that is still too much, thank God for the times you used to spend outside and know that in the whole scheme of things, weeds aren't the end of the world. As long as you are able, do what you can, even if it is just a few minutes a day. Ask God to help you enjoy the fresh air and sunshine, and think of all the people who would love to have a plot of earth to call their own.

The apostle Paul told the Philippians, **"Do everything without grumbling or arguing, so that you may become**

blameless and pure, 'children of God without fault in a warped and crooked generation'" (2:14,15).

The charge is to do everything without grumbling. Everything. Not some things. Not most of the time. Not when you and I are having a good day. Christians can stand apart in a warped and crooked world.

One of my dearest friends has been single for a long time. She recently met and fell in love with a godly man. A few days after she introduced him to her family and friends, the man had a seizure. Scans led to surgery, and surgery revealed a tumor that came back as stage 4 cancer. His life expectancy, apart from a miracle and an unbelievable response to treatment, is short.

I've watched my friend walk through this. Oh, there are tears. So many tears. And there are questions for sure. But she's so quick to point to God. She loves to say, "God is good" so that I can say, "all the time" so that she can say, "all the time" so that I can respond, "God is good!"

How can she continue to say this even as what she's been waiting for so long is plucked away? Where's the anger and "how could you, God?" Those conversations may still come, but right now the power of the Holy Spirit at work in her life is producing the fruit of the Spirit.

Grumbling comes easy. It is the way of our sinful nature, our default setting. If that's your go-to, you aren't worse than anyone else. You're just stuck in a rut. And the answer to getting out of the rut is to be in God's Word so the Spirit can infuse you with faith's fruit: love, joy, peace, patience, kindness, goodness, faithfulness, gentleness, and self-control.

Maybe start with the book of Acts. It chronicles the life of the apostle Paul. Paul endured more than most of us ever will. He was thrown out of synagogues and towns consistently. He was at times beaten, thrown in jail, even stoned and left for dead. He, more than anyone, had reason to complain. He had many opportunities to give up because nothing was easy.

In fact, in his second letter to the Corinthians, he appealed to God when something in his life, a thorn was how he referred to it, was keeping him from his full potential. You and I might think that God would agree wholeheartedly to remove that thorn so this man could do even more for the kingdom. After all, Paul was all in for God. If something would help him or something was hindering him, surely God would want to fix it. Right?

Well, no. Paul prayed three times, and finally God answered him, saying, **"My grace is sufficient for you, for my power is made perfect in weakness"** (2 Corinthians 12:9).

All too often, we pray for change, and change doesn't come. We can't imagine why God doesn't take our suggestions or make things better or move things into place so they are easier for us. God's answer just may be because his power and strength are even more evident in our weakness.

When things don't go our way, it doesn't mean God isn't listening. It certainly doesn't mean he doesn't care. It means that when he surveys the entire situation, he has decided in his perfect will that right now what we are asking will not serve us or him or others better.

When God gave Paul that answer, Paul said, **"Therefore I will boast all the more gladly about my weaknesses, so that Christ's power may rest on me"** (2 Corinthians 12:9).

He didn't pout or protest. He said that if God's answer was not to take away his thorn, then he would be weak so everyone who looked at him could see how strong God is.

Grumbling does not help the situation. It only makes it worse, because as we grumble, we're telling our brains to look for more things that aren't going well instead of focusing on how God is providing even now.

Maybe you aren't where you want to be. Maybe God hasn't answered your prayers the way you wanted or hoped. Grumbling doesn't point the world to God's goodness.

But waiting patiently will. So does praising God right where you are, even in the middle of the mess. "I'm praying and waiting on God" shows a firm confidence in God's faithfulness.

If like that woman who worked with me in the bakery you say, "But, Amber, you don't know what I've been through," I would agree. I don't. But Jesus said we have a Father in heaven who watches out for the birds and who tends the flowers. We are worth more to our Father than birds and flowers. And the apostle Paul assures us that whatever we go through—good or bad—will be used by God for good (Romans 8:28). Jesus promised that a day is coming when our days on earth will be over. He will take us to be with him in a place his Father, the Father who cares for us and knows the number of hairs on our heads, is preparing for us.

So let's commit our attitudes to the Lord. It will take time to unlearn the bad habits we've allowed in our lives, but everyone will be grateful when we decide to be pleasant and cheerful again. And it brings glory to our Father in heaven when we trust him.

Not long ago I was leading a class with women who were struggling with hurt. I asked them what words they used to describe themselves before the hurt. Their answers included: *kind, naive, friendly, hopeful.*

Then I asked them to come up with a word to describe themselves now. Some answers were: *angry, frustrated, scared, unfriendly.*

I assured them they didn't have to stay there. Healing puts us on a different path. It may be a long process. There may be steps to take to get to the point of releasing the grudge, forgiving, and learning to resolve the triggers. But we don't need to stay stuck, and we don't need to stay angry, broken, and wounded.*

We certainly can fight our temptations with God's help. In Christ we can live as new creations. Pray and ask God for the strength to do so. Find an accountability partner to encourage you when you want to give up. Set a small goal and stick to it, knowing that on the other side of this is a life that glorifies God.

---

* If you need help doing this, check out my book *Getting Past the Past: Reconciling What You Cannot Change*. It's available on Amazon.

Dip a toe in:

1. Have you ever walked away from a conversation and realized you didn't learn anything new about the other person because you didn't ask how they were or what was happening in their life? Try asking in your next conversation.

2. Have you ever known another person was going through a busy time but you didn't want to talk about it? Why?

3. What temptations do you struggle with?

4. Read Ephesians 4:28. What are the two reasons Paul gives for no longer stealing? How could those things help you overcome the temptations in your life?

5. Make a list of blessings. See if you can reach 100.

Chapter 3

Pray and Find People Who Pray

This probably seems like a no-brainer. Yet it's the thing so many of us forget to do, and then we wonder why things aren't the way we'd hoped. If you're longing for good, solid Christian relationships and aren't finding them, pray, pray some more, and then continue to pray. (Cue my mother quoting James anytime I would complain about anything: **"You do not have because you do not ask God"** [James 4:2].)

But how will you pray? Will you pray for a companion or someone to hold you accountable? Will you pray for a truth teller, someone who pushes you to do more than you otherwise would? Do you want someone who will help you grow spiritually? Are you looking for someone adventurous to travel with? Maybe what you want more than anything is an encourager or someone to hang out with right where you are.

Quite a few years ago, I started praying God would put people in my life who would help me be the best version of myself, friends who would hold me accountable and teach me things I didn't know. My desire at that time was to grow spiritually and professionally. I have not been disappointed.

Ten or fifteen years from now my prayers may be significantly different. But only God knows if I'll still be alive and what my situation will be at that time. Just today my husband and I had lunch with two women whose husbands went to be with the Lord, one after a very short illness and the other with almost no warning. Their lives and their needs changed significantly in a very short time.

One of the things we sometimes fail to pray for is to be the kind of friends whom the people we want to be around need. Good friendships occur when both people mutually encourage, help, and build each other up.

Pray–And

I have a theory about praying that I call "pray—and." It comes from Nehemiah 4:9: **"But we prayed to our God and posted a guard day and night to meet this threat."** Nehemiah is the name of a book in the Old Testament that chronicles a man named Nehemiah who restored the broken walls of Jerusalem. The walls were smashed when Judah was taken into captivity by King Nebuchadnezzer. At that time Babylon was the leading world power, so those who weren't killed during the takeover were taken as captives to Babylon.

Seventy years passed; eventually Babylon was conquered. As new kings came to power, they allowed the people to return to their homeland. The first wave to return focused on building a new temple to replace the one that was destroyed.

Almost 90 years after people began returning to Jerusalem, the walls of the city were still piles of rubble, a disgrace to Jerusalem and a sign of weakness to the neighboring people.

When Nehemiah, who worked as a cupbearer to a king in Susa (which was approximately 1,000 miles from Jerusalem), heard from his fellow countrymen about the condition of the walls, he asked the king if he could return to Jerusalem to repair the walls. He was granted permission and embarked on the four-month journey back to Jerusalem. Once there, he surveyed the damage and enlisted the help of those in Jerusalem to rebuild the walls.

When he undertook the project, some men from neighboring communities threatened violence. Nehemiah prayed, *and* he posted a guard. He didn't just pray. He didn't just post a guard. He prayed, *and* he took measures to be safe, much as we might pray that God keeps us safe while we simultaneously lock our doors and wear our seatbelts.

I don't know what your "and" is, but I'm guessing you and I have at least one thing that could be our "and." If you haven't gotten into the habit of reading your Bible, start there. Start in the New Testament if you want. Read one chapter a day or one section. Set a timer for five minutes; then work your way up from there. Say a quick prayer before you read that God would help you understand or that God would open your eyes to what he wants you to learn. You will learn many things about God when you read his Word, not the least of which is that he is a friend like no other. He loves you with everlasting love. He does not tire of your questions or weaknesses or failures. He's available every minute of every day and never rolls his eyes when you go back to him with the same thing on your heart.

Once you're in the habit of reading your Bible, another "and" could be reading other books. Being a lifelong learner is crucial not only to being interesting but also to being open to new experiences and adventures and understanding people. Just know that it's not about volume. I'm a purposely slow reader. I don't like to skim books. I prefer to take notes, underline, and absorb a book. Read at your own pace!

Maybe reading isn't your thing. Then make your "and" changing your algorithm. If you're not on social media, you might not know what I'm talking about. If you are on social media, your algorithm is the material (reels) that come your way based on your previous preferences, likes, and clicks. Social media sites take note of how much time you spend watching reels and which reels you like and share. If you've been consumed with politics, try hitting the heart to like an inspirational quote instead so you get more of those in your feed. If a pastor's video comes through as you're swiping and makes you think, like his post. Listen to podcasts and sermons that teach you something. When you do this, your algorithm changes, and you'll see more of these types of posts. Swipe quickly past the posts and reels that demean others or express a bad attitude.

Maybe the people you would like to be around most hike. Your "and" might be joining a hiking group. If you've always wanted to quilt, join a quilting group. One young woman I know started taking ballroom dance lessons. Pray and find your "and," the thing that would lead you to the people who are most like you.

Prayer groups

Maybe the group you need more than any other group is a group of people who pray. This is one activity I pray the church grabs onto more and more in the coming months and years, because prayer is powerful and changes so much.

Everyone I know is facing something hard. Maybe it's the decisions that have to be made about caring for elderly parents or a spouse. Maybe it's the challenges of raising children or a marriage that's stuck or the actions of a rebellious child. We all face decisions, hardships, and health issues from time to time. Most of us belong to churches, and those churches face their own battles. Prayer is our privilege as God's children. We can run to our heavenly Father anytime, any day and ask for help. And since he has a vantage point we don't, because he sees everyone's hearts and motives, he can answer our prayers in ways we wouldn't even know to consider.

You may be thinking that you can't imagine being vulnerable enough to tell other people about the struggles you or your family face. Are you desperate enough? That's what it took for me.

I had struggled with a situation one of my children was

going through for four and a half years. When some friends came over and opened up about the struggle their son was having, I decided right then and there that we needed to gather friends to pray. And we did. And things changed significantly for several of us in a very short amount of time. That was a year and a half ago. Not surprisingly, we haven't run out of things to pray about and still find we need to get together.

It is true that God hears the prayers of one person. Jesus' half brother James tells us the prayers of a righteous person are powerful and effective (James 5:16). But so are the prayers of community!

The early Christian church met often to pray. The book of Acts records several incidents involving prayer. Not long after Jesus ascended into heaven, King Herod had James, the brother of John and one of three disciples who comprised Jesus' inner circle, put to death. Seeing it pleased the Jews, Herod put Peter in prison. No doubt Herod intended that Peter would suffer the same fate as James.

Acts 12:5 tells us, **"So Peter was kept in prison, but the church was earnestly praying to God for him."**

The night before his trial, Peter was being guarded by four squads of four soldiers each. He was sleeping between two more soldiers and was bound by two chains. An angel entered the prison, woke Peter, and led him out of the prison and into the street. Once Peter was free, he made his way to the house of Mary, the mother of John Mark, **"where many people had gathered and were praying"** (Acts 12:12).

It was an impossible situation from an earthly perspective. Herod was known for being vicious. He found approval from the Jews when he killed James and would surely have killed Peter as well. Eighteen soldiers guarded Peter. No way Peter could walk out of there on his own. But the believers prayed, and the Lord responded.

In the very next chapter of the book of Acts, a man named Barnabas and Saul, who would soon be referred to as the apostle Paul, left on their first missionary journey. Before they left, the believers fasted and prayed, laid their hands on them (to bless them), and sent them off. God opened so many doors for them on that missionary journey.

In Acts chapter 16, Paul and his companion Silas were in prison praying and singing hymns when an earthquake opened the prison doors and shook the chains off of everyone. When the jailer drew his sword to take his life, Paul and Silas led the jailer to a relationship with Jesus.

Don't make the mistake of failing to pray. And when and if you want to get really serious about incredible things happening in the kingdom of God, gather believers and pray sincerely and earnestly. And see if those believers you pray with don't become friends you can go to at any time. Praying friends don't need much. They just need a text. My prayer warrior friends are like bloodhounds. If you send a text with an SOS, they'll check back in. They'll want to know how things are progressing, if anything has changed, and what the next need is.

What to pray for

Most of us are without excuse. Who can't pray? You don't need any athletic ability. You don't have to be smart or pretty or wealthy. You don't have to be eloquent. You just go to God, knowing he is the only one who can do what you are asking. With a believing heart, you ask him to intervene and change the things you can't.

While there's nothing wrong with praying for a person to be healed and for someone to pass a test or so and so to get the promotion they've applied for, it is far better to pray spiritually. Jesus asked, **"What good will it be for someone to gain the whole world, yet forfeit their soul?"** (Matthew 16:26).

If that person is healed but not walking with God, she has gained more time. But if she continues to refuse God's grace, her eternal outcome will be the same. And if he gets the promotion only to spend little to no time with his family and even less time with God, how has that been a blessing?

Far better to frame every request in light of a person's relationship to God.

- *Lord, work through this illness. God, work in her heart. As you heal her body, light a fire in her soul. Help the church use this opportunity to show Christian love and, in doing so, to show her your love. Amen.*

- *God, he is applying for this promotion. Only you know if this would be for his good. You know the people he would be working with and for. You know the demands that would be required of him. Even more important than money or position, we want him to serve you. If this position would put him in a place to do that, then please open the door. And if this would keep him from his family and keep him from working in your kingdom, if this position in any way would pull him away from you, then shut that door. Put godly people in his path, and let him be a godly influence to those you put in his path. Let his will be to follow you, and bless him in whatever way he can do that better. Amen.*

The blessing of having a group that regularly meets to pray spiritually for God's kingdom is that as you pray, you become more and more aware of the unbelievers around you and more and more in tune with praying for them in such a way that it opens a door to a conversation about God. Very often when things are not going well, people are grateful for anything you do to help them. When they tell you about an illness or job loss or putting the house on the market because they need to move closer to an ailing parent, you get the chance to step in and tell them you will be praying for them. And as you check back in, you can show them how God is answering prayers and tell them there is a God in heaven who loves them and cares about them.

My husband was a bedside nurse for years. Very often he told people that God had saved their lives because there was no medical reason they were still around. One man started asking my husband about his faith. By the power of the Holy

Spirit, Steve and some of the other Christian nurses led a man who had previously been a staunch atheist to a relationship with Christ in the days before his death. Do not hesitate to be bold in prayer and to tell someone about Jesus in these situations!

Don't forget to pray for your family. Don't think for a minute they aren't targets for the army of evil. A loving, praying Christian family is an enemy of Satan and his demonic army. And while they aren't responsible for everything that goes wrong in our lives—our own sinful desires bring plenty of trouble on our heads—they certainly take aim when they can. Sometimes we just end up in their cross fire. A family in turmoil can quickly become a relationship nightmare. When feelings are hurt, things can go quickly from bad to worse. Only God can keep everyone from falling apart and from chewing each other up. The prayers you pray for God to unite your family through hardship instead of letting it be a factor that divides everyone are prayers well prayed.

It is never a waste of time to pray for your family, to pray for your spouse and children to walk with God, to take his commands seriously, to be a godly influence, and to acquire godly influences. Pray for your children to marry believing spouses who are on fire for God, and pray that all of the spouses get along. That's a prayer you can pray your entire life as well as for God to keep making it happen long after you're gone. Pray your children don't get wrapped up in the things of the world but keep an eternal perspective. Pray that nothing enters their lives that causes them to lose their faith or dishonor God. If you pray these prayers and God is merciful and grants what you ask of him in this regard, your family will be a huge source of joy. You will enjoy being with them, and they will enjoy being with you. You will be a blessing to the Christian community and to any community because you will be loving God and loving people.

When the opposite happens, when there's strife and turmoil that rears its ugly head every holiday and birthday and anniversary and wedding and funeral, it takes an emotional toll on everyone. If that's your situation, you for sure need to consider gathering some people to pray that God fixes what you cannot.

God in his grace often gives us the spouses, friends, and relationships we ask for. But there isn't a relationship that won't go through hardships or frustrations. No one does or says the right things all the time. Sometimes our friends aren't there when we need them, and sometimes we aren't there for them. When you feel the tension in your relationships, and you will, pray that God mends what is broken. Pray your relationship survives the rough seasons and comes out stronger.

I have several friends who have been instrumental to a certain season of my life. Sometimes the seasons change, and those friends aren't as prominent as they once were. But over and over as we've had a chance to catch up, those friends prove our friendship isn't seasonal. We are at different stages for sure, and we don't see each other or talk like we used to, but a person who was once a good friend often knows enough about you that you can pick up the pieces where you left off. Pray for those friends as you see them on social media or as they come to mind. Never throw a good friend away. God alone knows when they will be back in your life again.

When my friend's spouse died, she sparked up several friendships with other friends who were widowed or divorced. She hadn't spent much time with them for years, but her new situation had her looking for advice and comfort, and she found it in women who were in a similar situation.

When you pray, you will find people who pray. And people who pray will always have things to pray for. And if you live as the apostle Paul advised when he said, **"Pray in the Spirit on all occasions with all kinds of prayers and requests. With this in mind, be alert and always keep on praying for all the Lord's people"** (Ephesians 6:18), you will notice things to pray about even when you aren't asked.

You will notice the mother looking worn out. You will notice the leader looking stressed. You will notice an elderly couple struggling. You will notice when someone hasn't been in church for a while. You will notice one of your children is moody.

Be alert, and you'll never cease to find reasons to pray.

Dip a toe in:

1. What is one spiritual blessing you would love to have (understanding the Scriptures better, Christian friends, a spouse who spurs you on spiritually, a church that's on fire for the things of God, etc.)?

2. What time of day are you most likely to pray?

3. Have you ever prayed out loud in front of other people? What scares you about doing so?

4. Buy a special journal and keep track of your prayers. Highlight the prayers as God answers them, realizing he doesn't always answer them the way you hope.

5. Read 1 Thessalonians 5:17. Which prayers have you quit praying?

6. Read Philippians 4:6. What are you most anxious about? That is the thing you need to pray about.

Chapter 4

Pursue the Relationships You Want

The word *pursue* means "to follow something or someone to catch them or it; to continue along a path or route." I don't know any relationship that goes well when it's coasting. Not our relationships with God, our marriages, our relationships with our children, and certainly not our relationships with our friends. If we want good relationships, we have to create space for them to happen.

Just the thought of that may put you on edge. By the time you finish working, get home, make supper, and put a load of laundry in, you're ready to tap out. Let me suggest that a whole lot of us are pursuing pseudorelationships and investing quite a lot of time in something that takes far more than it gives back.

Yes, relationships take effort

Here's an honest question: How much time do you spend scrolling; watching TV or movies; or listening to podcasts, audiobooks, or music?

Isn't it true that influencers on social media, our favorite characters on a series, or our favorite podcast hosts and musicians become pseudofriends to fill our relationship buckets? In some ways, that's an incredible blessing. When my kids were small, I had the Christian radio station on most days. The hosts of my favorite programs were "friends," offering Christian insight, encouragement, admonishment, and adult conversation at a time that I was at home with little people and unable to spend quality time with adults.

The same thing happened during the 2020 shutdowns. When my church and gym closed and I was laid off from my job as a private elderly companion, influencers became my people. Marie Kondo changed my life. *Vera*, a detective show on BritBox, offered my husband, Steve, and me a distraction on Steve's days off when he worked on a COVID floor with COVID patients at a time when we weren't sure how deadly it was. My then 12-year-old daughter and I watched another detective series twice over the course of 2020 and 2021.

While distractions are useful at times and influencers can teach you things to improve your life, our devices can't replace real relationships. The American Medical Association identified loneliness and isolation as a public health risk in June 2023 following the attorney general's May 2023 advisory on the epidemic of loneliness and social isolation. As much as we were on our devices during 2020–2022, and a lot of us were on our devices more than we had ever been before, it didn't fill our relationship needs. In fact, we were lonelier than ever. And the results on physical health were devastating.

In plain English: Your phone and TV can't replace a real person smiling at you, touching your hand, listening to your concerns, and laughing with you about the silly things in life. You need real people. And if that feels like it's more work than it's worth, it's because the counterfeit is always cheaper and easier. What is real and lasting and worthwhile will require effort, but the effort of friendship will pay exponentially.

What does that effort look like? It may look like being the one to organize an event, text everyone, and coordinate schedules. I've heard of people throwing in the towel because they're always the one to initiate. But maybe that's your role. A friend group doesn't need four organizers. It needs one, and if that's you, embrace it!

A great majority of the time, I am the initiator. I plan wedding showers and baby showers for the relatives. I plan holiday gatherings and meals with my children. And I plan outings with my two friends who are in their late 70s and early 80s. I text my friends to see who can walk when and when coffee will work with my friends who prefer to sit rather than walk.

Not long ago a friend and I both had to be at the same meeting. I had a bunch of other responsibilities that day and the next but knew we would both be staying overnight. I reached out and asked if we could walk in the morning before she headed back home and I started my next round of responsibilities. She was happy to oblige. I don't often get time with this friend, so even though we both had busy schedules, I hated the idea of not spending time together if we could make it work. It was a simple thing to text, and I wouldn't have been upset if she had said it just didn't fit into her schedule. But it did, and it made for a wonderful memory. Just yesterday when I was in the same area, walking down the same street with other people, I was remembering the wonderful time we had together.

Worst-case scenario, they don't answer the phone or text or call back. At least you tried. Just recently a good friend went through an insanely busy time. In the course of six months, I reached out four or five times, but she wasn't able to make any of my offers work. Finally, we found a time that worked for both of us, and though it was short, it was fruitful and so fulfilling. It happened because I didn't stop reaching out. That same friend and another friend are speaking at the same event I am in a few days. We asked the venue to get a suite for us so we can all be together. We could get three hotel rooms, but man, we've found the rich memories happen in the conversations just before bed or while reading our Bibles together and praying.

When a dear friend died unexpectedly a year ago, I picked one of my other friends up at her house. We drove to the wake and funeral together. It was such a blessing to be together, working out our emotions and sharing memories. That night we sat on our beds with open Bibles crying out to God in prayer. The next day before the funeral, we walked around the hotel parking lot praying for our friend's family, for the church, for the hole she would be leaving in ministry.

Earlier this year a friend asked if she could crash in my hotel room when we were both going to be at the same conference. Both of us had busy schedules, but having her with me ended up being such a blessing. We read the Bible together, prayed together, and sorted the days out together. It made the event exponentially better, and it happened because she asked and I was open to sharing my life and time with her.

It's easy to fall into complacency or to think that maybe you will be a bother and shouldn't get in someone's way. But consider Mary the mother of Jesus. When the angel Gabriel came to her and told her she would have a baby, he also told her that Elizabeth, her relative, was going to have a baby in her old age (Luke 1:36).

Mary could have heard that information, thought how nice for Elizabeth, and gone on with her life. Instead, she got ready and hurried to Elizabeth's house, where she stayed for three months. Think of the blessing that was! Both Elizabeth and Mary had miraculous pregnancies. Elizabeth was old and barren. A child was an answer to many years of praying, but surely Elizabeth never expected to be pregnant at that point in life. Mary was engaged, but she wasn't married. For her a baby was an impossibility since she hadn't been intimate with a man.

Elizabeth's husband, Zechariah, hadn't been able to speak throughout her pregnancy because when Gabriel announced that his wife would have a baby, Zechariah struggled to believe it could happen. Gabriel told Zechariah:

> **"I am Gabriel. I stand in the presence of God, and I have been sent to speak to you and to tell you this good news. And now you will be silent and not able to speak until the day this happens, because you did not believe my words, which will come true at their appointed time."** (Luke 1:19,20)

Elizabeth was finally pregnant after waiting her whole life for a child, and by now she was **"very old"** (Luke 1:7). Her husband couldn't talk. Besides all that, she remained in seclusion during the first five months of her pregnancy. The Bible doesn't tell us why, but it isn't hard to imagine why she might have gone that route. How do you explain a pregnancy at that age? How do you begin to explain that an angel appeared and announced your child and that the child had a special purpose connected to the long-awaited Messiah?

Elizabeth was one of the few people who knew and understood exactly what Mary was going through with this new unexpectant pregnancy. Gabriel planted the seed, and Mary took hold of it. She leaned on Elizabeth for encouragement and support, and they mutually walked through the mystery of it together. It took effort from both women, Mary to get to Elizabeth and Elizabeth to open her home, but oh how they would benefit from the effort.

Step out of isolation

Before I move on, I'm afraid you might remain in your

bubble because you've convinced yourself, or the devil himself or one of his minions has planted the seed and watered it in your mind, that no one would want to be around you. You routinely tell yourself that you are too ugly, fat, stupid, overwhelming, emotional, old, awkward, fill in the blank with your demeaning word of choice. And maybe there are habits that you need to get under control. Do you want to know a great way to do that? By being around people who have mastered those things AND by being open to learning their lifestyle adaptations to make that happen.

It's a common misconception that you need to get yourself together in order to get A, B, or C. In truth, being around people who are the type of person you want to be can be the greatest motivation and inspiration. This is referred to as the spillover effect. One article by senior editor of *KelloggInsight*, Emily Stone, explains that if you are within 25 feet of a high achiever, your own performance tends to go up. But being around a negative person can be exponentially more dangerous. "While positive spillover was limited to about a 25-foot radius, with toxic workers, 'you can see their imprint and negative effect across an entire floor.'"[6]

Here's what that means to you. It's well worth the effort it takes to get out of your space, because too often the space where you feel most comfortable is also the place where you bombard yourself with toxic thoughts and self-hatred. The longer you stay there, the harder it is to get out of it.

Some people do really well working from home. They are

self-motivated and thrive in their own working environment. But a whole lot of people found the opposite to be true when they were sent home in 2020. For some people, it was especially catastrophic as they interacted with fewer and fewer people, and the problems of the world became bigger because they weren't out seeing people every day and experiencing the things that make you smile, breathe deeply, and thank God that you are alive.

It is easy and convenient to stay home. But easy and convenient might not be best. I stayed home 24/7 from March 2020 to September 2021. If it weren't for shear desperation due to financial circumstances, I probably wouldn't have gotten the courage to walk into a nursing home an hour from home and do that first shift. But that was exactly what I needed. Being around people again and having a reason to get ready were just two benefits of getting out of the house. It's amazing how much more exercise you get just walking from your car to the building and from the office to the bathroom after being confined to a house where everything is within a few cubic feet. Exercise and sunlight and being around people can change so much if you let it.

Pursuing relationships will require effort, but the advantages far outweigh the consequences of staying in the same place. And staying in the same place because it's convenient and you have lost all confidence in yourself is not going to get you out of your situation. It may take a lot of effort initially to get out of your house and back into society, but that's only because you've gotten used to isolation. If you take a step and reintroduce yourself into an environment where you'll see people regularly, that will become your new normal again.

There are things I don't miss about working in a nursing home (the one hour drive each way on a sometimes treacherous road in the winter being the most prevalent), but there's a lot I miss. I miss camaraderie with my coworkers, the exercise, and speaking hope into the residents.

It's easy to get stuck in comfortable without noticing your demise. Start thinking and praying now about how you can pursue relationships, not only for your own benefit but also for the benefit of others. Perhaps you have found a way to be a light to others from home. If so, then God bless you!

Being around other people is a way for you to meet people you'd otherwise never meet. It's a chance to be a light, to show others Jesus. If you are open to conversations and pick up on the hints others throw your way, you will have ample opportunities to pray for and with other people. Don't just think about this and move on. *Look and pray for opportunities* to tell people about Christ. Look for places to volunteer; ask a neighbor to coffee. Look for opportunities to connect with people you'd otherwise never know.

Trust me when I tell you this is likely to be a challenge for all of us. I like to get things done. I'm driven, and my to-do lists are always considerably longer than I can accomplish. I am recklessly unaware of the amount of time things take, and I'm prone to tunnel vision when I'm in the zone. All too often I haven't stopped to give someone my full attention and figured it out AFTER a missed opportunity. But I'm working on it.

A while back I asked my sister for advice about something. She listened and then asked, "What would 80-year-old Amber be glad that you did?" That shapes a lot of my decision-making these days. I've been around a lot of 80-year-olds. Most 80-year-olds know the work will always be there. When you finish one project, you'll start another. You do the dishes and clean the floor and make food, and you're good until the next time you eat. At the end of your life, the vast majority of people do not resent the time they spent with their families. They don't resent the time they invested in other people. They value relationships over material possessions.

We all have things to do. Some seasons are harder than others. But relationships are worth pursuing—chasing after. So here are just a few ideas for you to start.

Dip a toe in:

1. If you've been watching church online, start going in person once a month with a goal of eventually returning most weeks. Make a point to greet one person. Find out their name and something about them.

2. Join a group Bible study. Maybe a small group is too much at first; you aren't quite ready to be one of 10 or 12 people. How about going to a Sunday-morning Bible study

and talking to the person next to you? Ask if they have any pets. Trust me on this. Pet people love talking about their pets, and people who don't have pets are usually pretty passionate about why they don't (anymore).

3. Next time you go to the store, hold the door open for someone or smile at someone who is walking down the aisle near you.

4. Wave to your neighbor and ask how they've been lately.

5. Pray and ask God to show you what changes you could make to be friendlier and to have access to people who would enrich your life. Then pray for the strength to make those changes!

6. Look for a place to volunteer one or two days a week. Consider a local animal shelter, hospital, or courthouse. As you volunteer, you will likely find plenty of people to encourage and pray for.

Chapter 5

Pursue Godly Living

You might think pursuing righteousness—right living, godly living—has nothing to do with relationships. That notion couldn't be further from the truth. In fact, more than anything, this will determine the kind of friends you have. It will mean finding friends who put God's way first. Yes, that might keep you from having as many friends. But the friends you have will be better than having lots of friends because you were willing to cut moral corners.

If you drink at the high school party, you will fit in. If you go to the party but don't drink, you might not be invited next time. If you stand up for the kid everyone else is mocking, you won't be the life of the party. In fact, you may be the next object of ridicule.

But here's what we so often miss. Going along with the crowd might make us popular for a time but often not with the kind of friends who want the best for us. The party crowd is always up for a good time, sometimes taking things too far, but once you follow God's will regarding drunkenness and decide that you need to study more, take care of yourself, or save money, they quickly lose interest. Certain high achievers (not all high achievers), some competitive sports people (not all competitive sports people), the people who are all about looks, and anyone who finds value in what they do or how they look rather than in their identity in God love you being part of the group until you question if there's more or quit going out of your way to accommodate them or decide something they do isn't in your best interest.

True friends want the best for you. They want you to grow and do more than you imagine you can do, but only if that means doing it God's way. Sometimes God's way is doing less to serve more. Moms who care for small children or the spouse who is caring for their no-longer-able spouse know they *could* do so much more.* They could work and earn good money and go out with friends and travel and enjoy pleasures. Or for a season, they could adjust their priorities to care for the ones who need them. True friends understand seasons. They will text when you aren't able to leave your home or call you during nap time so you can have adult conversation. They will cheer for you as you do the things of God, pray for you, and help you refocus when you start to wonder if serving in this way is worth it.

Psalm 1:1,2 says, **"Blessed is the one who does not walk in step with the wicked or stand in the way that sinners take or sit in the company of mockers, but whose delight is in the law of the Lord, and who meditates on his law day and night."**

---

* That is not to say that every person is a caretaker, and sometimes a person requires more care than you can give. In those situations, finding good care is the most loving thing you can do.

Note the person who is considered blessed. He or she meditates, thinks about, focuses on the law of God day and night. God's Word isn't a Sunday morning thing. The person who is blessed is intent on knowing God, understanding his ways, and walking in them.

If you decide to live this way, your circle might get smaller. When you are convinced that God knows best and has your best in mind, that will be both foreign and unacceptable to a lot of people. You won't go to the same places and do the same things that everyone else is. That concert with the artist that glorifies sin? Probably not where you want to spend your money. That new house in the new subdivision may not fit into your budget if you are set on giving to church and giving to help those less fortunate. The club sport for your kids may not fit into your schedule, budget, or priorities for your family if it means you can't make it to church, you'll be strapped to give, and you'll spend all your time at the field or court at the expense of other priorities.

The biblical prophet Daniel was an old man when he was called to read some writing that appeared on a wall in the Babylonian king's palace. This was a time in the Bible when God's people, the Israelites, had been taken captive by the Babylonians. Daniel had spent his life serving God and the government. The writing appeared when the king and a thousand of his nobles were eating and drinking. The king ordered that the sacred goblets from the temple in Jerusalem be brought out so he and his nobles and concubines could drink from them. As they did, **"they praised the gods of gold**

and silver, of bronze, iron, wood and stone" (Daniel 5:4).

They praised stuff. They marveled at the buildings, their banquet halls, temples, architecture, houses. It's only after the writing appeared that we realize Daniel wasn't part of this celebration. But that shouldn't surprise us. Daniel chapters 1-4 show Daniel and his friends Shadrach, Meshach, and Abednego's involvement in the government. They had been carried off to Babylon from Jerusalem as teens and put in Nebuchadnezzar's three-year program to train them in Babylonian culture, religion, and sciences. From the very beginning, they set themselves apart from the group. First, they resolved not to eat the food the others ate. It wasn't prepared according to the regulations of their ceremonial law, and food in Babylon was often eaten in honor of one of their many gods.

Daniel and his friends had been taught to eat according to God's law, and even when they were taken from their homeland and put in another living situation altogether, they chose to honor God with what they ate and drank. It certainly wasn't easier for them to do so. The food they refused was choice food: good, rich, pleasing, exquisite, and delectable.

If you've ever been on a cruise, you may have an idea of the kind of food Daniel and his friends turned down. I have only been on one cruise, but as I talk to others, it seems par for the course on cruises that the food is exquisite and abundant. Lunch and dinner weren't the potpies, tacos, soups, salads, or sandwiches I usually make. There were several courses, and each course was made with fresh ingredients and presented with care. I consumed combinations of spices and creams and desserts unlike anything I've heard of: things like sweet potato ginger soup and tiny individual chocolate bowls filled with chocolate mousse and drizzled with melted chocolate.

That is no doubt the kind of food Daniel and his friends refused, choosing instead to ingest only vegetables and water. There's no way that the other young people from other nations who were in the same program didn't look at Daniel and his friends as freaks. Who would give up all the delicacies for vegetables?

If you refuse to consume what others are consuming—excessive alcohol, drugs, or whatever—your peers may think you're crazy. You may be left out. You might find yourself like me at 16 years old, alone in a hostel in Germany while everyone else in my group went to a festival to get drunk.

But Daniel and his friends didn't limit their dedication to God to consumption. In Daniel chapter 3, Shadrach, Meshach, and Abednego refused to bow down to worship King Nebuchadnezzar's statue. And in case you're thinking that's a no-brainer, let's revisit the scene. Nebuchadnezzar called together all the nobles, advisors, and important people and had them stand before the statue and commanded them to bow. Of the hundreds, possibly thousands, of people present, three refused.

When I was 21, I went to Vietnam on a global studies program through my university. While there, we visited a

Buddhist temple. As we passed a statue of Buddha, our tour guide bowed, and so did the next person in our group and the next and the next and the next. I was near the back of our group, and my poetry professor was next to me. He turned and asked, "Is everyone Buddhist now?"

I did not bow when I entered the temple, but I understand how easy it is to do, even without a clearly defined threat. Shadrach, Meshach, and Abednego were not only threatened but thrown into a fiery furnace because of their conviction.

And that's exactly what life is going to feel like a whole lot of the time when you do things God's way. It will force you to be odd man out, sometimes (and you don't want to hear this anymore than I want to say it) even with other Christians. Not everyone is on the same journey you are on. All of us grow and mature at a different pace. And sometimes the things you choose to do in the name of having freedom in Christ are going to be against someone else's conscience and vice versa.

I have had maybe five alcoholic drinks since I was 22 years old. I realized early in my drinking experiences that witty one-liners came pretty easily when my filter was relaxed. I decided I didn't want to be the person everyone preferred drunk. When I tried to drink between pregnancies, getting up in the morning after even just one or two drinks was not fun. For me to be the kind of mom I wanted to be, one who woke up ready to take care of kids, I realized alcohol wouldn't be part of the equation.

If you choose not to drink, there's a good chance you're not going to be invited to certain events. Some people won't sit by you or want to be around you. You will be perceived as different at times.

Now let's return to the writing on the wall as recorded in Daniel chapter 5. Daniel was called to interpret the writing and promised purple clothes, a gold chain, and the third-highest position in the kingdom if he did. This is what he said:

> **Then Daniel answered the king, "You may keep your gifts for yourself and give your rewards to someone else. Nevertheless, I will read the writing for the king and tell him what it means.**
>
> **"Your Majesty, the Most High God gave your father Nebuchadnezzar sovereignty and greatness and glory and splendor."** (Daniel 5:17,18)

Daniel wasn't partaking of the revelry. He had to be summoned to get the interpretation, and clearly he wasn't interested in the things the king thought he would desire. Yet Daniel wasn't rude. He didn't act with an air of being better than them. He showed honor to the king, referring to him as "Your Majesty."

If our pursuit of righteousness brings us to a place of pride, we've missed the goal entirely. If the choices we make because of our consciences condemn others for making different choices, we've missed the goal entirely. I don't drink, but I don't expect my Christian brothers and sisters to abstain from drinking. I certainly don't think I'm better because I've made a different choice than they have. I have found what works for me, and it's up to each of them to discover what works for them. If they want my opinion, I'm happy to give it. If not, I'm happy to keep it to myself. If they want to be around me, I'm happy to be around them. And if my convictions keep them from wanting to be near me, I'm okay with that too.

Jesus said we are the light and the salt of the world. Our role is to love others and pray for them and be prepared to tell them why we do what we do. That's not to say they'll agree with us or appreciate our decisions.

One traveling nursing assistant told me her goal was to have sex with a white man during her short assignment at our nursing home. She had her eye on two male nurses. When I told her the only man I had ever had sex with was my husband, she nearly fell over. She had never met anyone in her entire 20-some years of life who had only had one sex partner.

"Seriously, why?"

I explained to her that even though Steve and I don't always get it right either, sex in a marriage is a whole different concept than casual sex. It's commitment and taking care of one another and stability, and some studies show that it makes for the most rewarding sex life. And that isn't too hard to understand. The more partners you have, the more you have to compare.

I'm pretty certain I was the object of a whole string of comments in her text threads that night. But she had something to think about, and for the first time ever, she was introduced to someone who viewed sex differently than anyone she'd ever met.

Maybe it didn't mean anything to her in that moment, or maybe it did. Maybe it meant something to someone she talked to about it. Maybe they looked into it more or thought about it or decided to do something different.

Either way, when you pursue a godly life, two things become clear. You will stand apart. And if you are winsome about it instead of judgmental, you may get the opportunity to tell someone why you live the way you do. What they do with that is ultimately not your concern. Only the Holy Spirit can change hearts.

It's the way Jesus lived. He walked the streets. He stopped for people who needed healing. He ate with sinners. He went to dinner at the houses of tax collectors. He didn't revel in sin, but he didn't stay away from sinners either.

He also had his closest friends—Peter, James, and John—who loved the Lord and sought his will. They were beside him in his earthly ministry. Jesus entered the space of sinners. He made himself available so they could learn about his ways. But he also guarded his heart and spent most of his time with those who knew his mission (albeit not entirely) and supported his work.

There's plenty to do in the interim of waiting for the relationships you crave. If you're single and looking for a spouse, become the spouse you think the man or woman of your dreams would want. If you want a husband who's on fire for the Lord, get into the Word. Meditate on it. Live it. Join Bible studies and the worship team or the group at church that does whatever you are equipped to do. If you want your spouse to be healthy and strong, then become healthy and strong. Learn how to cook healthy meals. Join a gym or buy some weights; canoe or take trips with friends who push your endurance. If your ideal spouse is organized, sharpen your cleaning skills. An organized man or woman probably won't be attracted to someone who keeps a slovenly living space.

The same concept applies to the friendships you are craving. While you wait, become the person your ideal friend would want to hang out with. As I wrote more books and spoke at more conferences, I desired friends who actively did ministry. I'm happy when I travel to stay after and take walks or have coffee with other women in ministry. As people get to know me, they introduce me to their friends and tell me to connect with other people who share the same passions I do.

All of us in God's kingdom need to be on the lookout for people we can mentor and shepherd. When you see people in the younger generation, mentor them, teach them how to act and behave and make decisions that glorify God. Tell them the mistakes you have made so they can learn without having to make the same mistakes.

And as you pursue righteousness, keep your eyes open for those who are weak in their faith and/or struggling.

Shepherd them through the tough times, and build them up so they can get back on their feet. You may find this hard to believe, but as you mentor the youth and shepherd the weak, you will be building relationships that will bless you.

Dip a toe in:

1. If you're not sure what you could or should do differently to live God's way, go through the Ten Commandments listed below and decide which one(s) you want to work on.

    a. Do you live in such a way that God is number one in your life? Do you spend time in his Word every day and in prayer?

    b. Do you misuse his name, either by using it as a curse word or by saying you are a Christian but misrepresenting him by the way you act?

    c. Do you make church a priority? Is the Word of God read and taught in your living environment?

    d. Do you respect and submit to authority? Do you complain about people in government, those who run the church, or your boss instead of praying for them and encouraging them?

    e. How many people do you hate? Who drives you nuts? Whom do you think you are better than? Do you appreciate life at every age and work to make sure those who are vulnerable get the care they need?

f. Do you view sex as something reserved for marriage? Do you avoid sexual images and programs? Do you keep yourself from lusting after others?

g. Do you take what isn't yours? Do you steal people's time or do other things when you should be working?

h. Do you talk badly about others? Do you put people down?

i. Do you look at what others have and get jealous, wondering why you don't have it?

j. Do you look at your neighbor or friend and envy his/her spouse, property, or children instead of thanking God for your situation whatever it is?

2. What do you need to work on most: your thoughts, words, or actions?

3. Which of your friends would hold you accountable?

Chapter 6

Get Involved

I notoriously don't know where to find things in the Bible. I usually can recite a passage or at least a halfway decent paraphrase, but when it comes to the reference (what book and chapter of the Bible the passage is found), I'm mostly dependent on Google. There are a few exceptions, including one of my all-time favorite sections of the Bible, which I already referenced in chapter 1.

> **They devoted themselves to the apostles' teaching and to fellowship, to the breaking of bread and to prayer. Everyone was filled with awe at the many wonders and signs performed by the apostles. All the believers were together and had everything in common. They sold property and possessions to give to anyone who had need. Every day they continued to meet together in the temple courts. They broke bread in their homes and ate together with glad and sincere hearts, praising God and enjoying the favor of all the people. And the Lord added to their number daily those who were being saved.** (Acts 2:42-47)

If we were studying this section together, I would have you circle the words *all, everyone, anyone* and *every. All* the believers were together. They (all the believers) gave to *anyone* who had need. *Every* day they (all the believers) met, ate, and praised God.

Who devoted themselves to the study of Scripture? Who got together? Who helped out? Who gave? Read it with me: *All the believers.*

That means you. Whether you've been a believer your whole life or this is the first Christian book you've read, if you believe that Jesus is your Savior who died to take away your sins, you are included in everyone, all, anyone, every. The best way to experience Christianity and the best way to grow in your Christian faith is to be with other believers. And this section in Scripture offers a pretty good description of how to do that.

1. The Acts chapter 2 church devoted themselves to the apostles' teaching.

The apostles used the Old Testament Scriptures to show that Jesus was the promised Messiah and that he was the Messiah they were waiting for. The Pharisees and teachers of the law had presupposed errantly that the Messiah would be an earthly ruler who would establish a physical earthly kingdom, similar in power and popularity to King David's.

If you want to form solid relationships with other believers, gather with a group devoted to the teaching of Scripture. Sunday morning worship is a start for sure, but if the only time you're getting in the Bible is a 20- to 30-minute sermon once a week, you will miss all that comes with gathering with others to study the Word.

I've been teaching the Bible for 21 years. I've led numerous women's Bible studies and taught a young adult's group. I've taught high schoolers and countless Sunday school and Bible history classes. I wouldn't know how many church groups I've spoken to or how many conferences or events I've spoken at, but here's what I know. Something special happens as we gather around the Word of God. The Holy Spirit binds hearts and minds. Friendships form. Tears flow; laughter resounds. People who didn't know each other at all feel a connection to other people in the room.

And that's secondary to the greatest blessings. When you study God's Word, you are connecting to God. His Spirit is at work to guide and direct you and to connect you to the source of life. You will read and see the hundreds of affirmations God gives in his Word. Page after page attests to his love for his people and his interaction in their lives. God is the master of encouragement. We, like our biblical ancestors, so often see and feel our humanity; we are well acquainted with our weaknesses and understand we aren't enough. That was never an obstacle for God. Over and over, he assured his people they didn't have to be strong or smart or above average. He assured them he would compensate for any of their deficiencies.

He compensates for our deficiencies too. I'm so glad I don't have to depend on my own strength, competence, or prowess, because they run out routinely. As I'm in God's Word, I'm reminded how he worked in his people's lives in the past. And because he tells us he's the same yesterday, today, and forever, I know he will do the same for me today and tomorrow and until I take my last breath. I know when you go to him, he will do the same for you.

There are so many blessings in studying with other people. It's a blessing to study with people who have studied the Bible a long time. They often know contextual and historical information and the meanings of Bible words that if you're new to the Bible might seem foreign. They can explain how this section of Scripture ties into a different part of the Bible.

But that's not to take anything away from our new-to-the-faith brothers and sisters. Reading the Bible with a new believer allows us to see and marvel at things we've gotten used to. It reminds us how the Spirit has opened our eyes to things that aren't immediately apparent.

When I read the Bible with others, they pick up on things I would otherwise miss. And because each of us has different struggles, the things they catch may just convict me in all the right ways. Their struggles aren't necessarily mine and vice versa. They may point out casually that a certain passage is a reminder that the things of the earth promise so much but deliver so little, while the things of God promise and deliver what the world could never give. And because they are steadfast in God's Word and quit falling for the gimmicks of the world a long time ago, they move on.

But what they said in passing leaves a lasting impression on me because I'm still struggling in that area.

While studying the Bible with others, we can be encouraged because we all have different spiritual gifts. The encouragers will find encouraging things in the passages we read. Those who are gifted to serve notice the people who serve. Leaders make observations about the style and effectiveness of leadership used. Those gifted in artistic ways see the passage or account as a big picture or connect it to a bigger, overarching theme. It's an incredible unfolding of Scripture and powerful to see God at work so intimately in his people then and now.

If you're new to the Bible and just want to stay under the radar and learn for a while before gathering with other Christians, a good place to start may be a large Sunday Bible study between services. But I hope you don't stay there.

I've led many women's Bible studies, and while it's true that not every group meshes, studying the Bible together and praying for each other is only the start. We also ask each other for advice, direction, and help. We bear each other's burdens and walk together much as the people did in Acts chapter 2.

In fact, several years ago during our women's Bible study, I received the text that one of the women who had attended the study faithfully for years had gone to be with the Lord. She had been battling cancer for a long time, and we had been praying her through. We knew at the beginning of our meeting that night that she was in her last hours. We thought it was perfectly wonderful that the Lord took her home during our normal meeting time and rejoiced that her suffering was over. Our study was, after all, almost like experiencing the smallest speck of heaven: to meet together and read; learn with other believers; to worship, pray, and encourage one another.

My husband and I have been part of an in-home Bible study group for the past 20 years or so. That too has been an influential part of our Christian walk. The people we've studied the Bible with have become our closest friends. They are the people we text when we're struggling. They are the ones who will show up with food when someone's had surgery, who check in on us if we've got something going on. Even more than that, they're the people who have modeled Christian marriage for us. And because Steve and I are the youngest couple in the group, we've learned so much about parenting from our friends. Being part of a small group was a major contributor to recognizing and determining our family values. Our friends mentored us through tough seasons and pulled back the curtain and let us into their struggles so we could learn from them as we encouraged and supported them.

And if for some reason none of those things are offered or appeal to you, then consider starting a small group Bible study with a handful of your friends. Invite two or three others over or to a coffee shop, pick a book of the Bible or one of the many topical Bible studies available, and make it happen.

If any part of you desires to have the kind of relationships Acts chapter 2 describes, being part of a Bible study, whether large or small, is a key factor. It's too important to neglect and gives far more than it takes.

So I don't set you up for despair and disappointment, know this: If for whatever reason you don't find your people, try a different group. Go to the church across town. Start a different in-home Bible study. Ask around to see if there's another women's or men's study. I've started several Bible studies. Sometimes the people didn't mesh. I've had a few women at different times stop coming to a class because someone else was coming, and there were unresolved issues. Hopefully in time they worked it out. I also stopped a women's Bible study once because one of the women coming was divisive and was undermining my leadership. When it came time to plan the next study, I simply said I was going to take a break. The Lord took care of the rest.

2. The Acts chapter 2 church helped each other and those in need.

My new friend Bridget has had a heart for missions for years. She's gone on several mission trips and taken several people with her over the years. She really wanted to go to India to help women stuck in sex trafficking. So she researched how to make it happen, talked with several Christian organizations, and finally found one who would work with her. Then she started gathering the women who would go with her. She's gone twice now, taken different friends, and is thrilled at the doors God is opening for her and her work.

It started as an idea for her, and she asked around and found other women who were willing to help. I have had similar experiences on a much smaller scale. We have low-income housing—both apartments and trailer courts—not far from our church, so I wanted to have a garage "sale" where people could come and get whatever they wanted or needed for free. Once church leadership approved it, others enthusiastically helped. Many people brought items. Others showed up to sort, while others were on hand the day of the sale. Still others helped take it down.

If God puts something on your heart, start asking questions, and see who rallies around you. You may meet some of the most incredibly amazing people. You don't have to go to India or plan something on a huge scale. You could ask if anyone wants to visit people in a local nursing home or write letters or send care packages to college students.

And if you aren't a planner or an idea person, no worries! Just show up when others let you know of an opportunity. I have a friend who volunteers at a hospice. That's not a place where everyone would feel comfortable, but what a blessing to serve the families of people who are dying. Every time I'm at my local hospital, I see volunteers. I flew to Montana a few days ago. An older gentleman who volunteers at the airport made my few minutes waiting for a tram very enjoyable.

There's work to be done in small churches and small communities as well as in large churches and large communities. When your pastor sends an email asking for help, help if you are able. When you read in the church newsletter that they need people to serve at a funeral or move chairs or man the booth at the county fair, do what you can. Will every call for service be your thing? No. We all have our spiritual gifts, personality characteristics, and physical abilities. But sometimes you just need to think outside the box or look for what needs to be done.

I do not have a good singing voice, but I love contemporary Christian music. My church didn't offer any contemporary music at any of our worship services. After meeting with the pastor and worship coordinator and finding they weren't opposed to it, I gathered some musicians and unofficially became the praise band director. I schedule practices, pick the music, attend rehearsals, and make sure everyone knows what they're doing.

I could have shrugged my shoulders and waited for someone else to do something. (In fact, that was my course of action for a long time.) I could have lamented week after week that we only sang one kind of music at church. Or I could see an opportunity and take advantage of the opportunity, and in doing so, spend time a couple times a month with people at the church I otherwise wouldn't have the opportunity to see.

Bottom line: If you're lonely, get involved somewhere doing something. And if you don't know where to start, consider your passions. Do you have a heart to help young women in difficult situations? Volunteer at a local pregnancy resource center. Do you care about senior citizens? Volunteer at a nursing home or a hospice. Do you care about the weak? Consider visiting shut-ins. If your kids are in school, consider volunteering at the school. (I've never been in a school that didn't want volunteers.) Consider being part of one of the many committees that meet at church.

We have women on the altar guild who place flowers on the altar, set up and take down Lord's Supper, and change the paraments (the cloth on the pulpit representing different church seasons). We have a fellowship committee, evangelism committee, youth committee, adult spiritual growth committee, stewardship committee. There are multiple ways to serve depending on your interests and gifts. Each of those committees meets regularly, plans events, and works to put the events on. Every event offers opportunities to work with the other members of the committee, form friendships, and feel like a valued member of the body of Christ.

If you are not at a place in life where you can help at all, consider showing up. Showing up is a gift to those who put the work in to do something.

A few years ago, I attended a presentation at a local church put on by a missionary about his travels. I sat down next to a woman, and we quickly struck up a conversation. She was a friendly older woman, and we had a delightful evening together. A few months later, I saw her again at a different church for a different church function. Again, we talked. A year or so later, I was at an entirely different church, and you guessed it, I ran into this woman. She made a point to be at the events going on around our church community. She was old and struggled to walk, so she couldn't help out in any way. But she showed up, and as she showed up, she was able to be around others, engage in conversation, and enjoy the company of people rather than sitting home alone.

I have another friend who lives in a senior living facility. Her health is not allowing her to go out much anymore. But she makes a point to go to their Bible study when she can and possibly to their coffee hour a couple times a week. Even though it's not easy for her, she recognizes the importance of getting out of her apartment in order to see other people.

It's easy to fall into complacency when you've lost touch with others. It's easy to complain when you aren't actively working within an organization. For years when I was volunteering in several positions at the church, anytime anyone came to me with complaints, I invited them to come help me. Several did. And they found it wasn't as easy as they thought. Once you get into the trenches, you realize the limitations and how much you could do if you had another six arms and more people with ideas.

Let me end this section with this from the book of Exodus

> **Then Moses said to the Israelites, "See, the Lord has chosen Bezalel son of Uri, the son of Hur, of the tribe of Judah, and he has filled him with the Spirit of God, with wisdom, with understanding, with**

> **knowledge and with all kinds of skills—to make artistic designs for work in gold, silver and bronze, to cut and set stones, to work in wood and to engage in all kinds of artistic crafts. And he has given both him and Oholiab son of Ahisamak, of the tribe of Dan, the ability to teach others. He has filled them with skill to do all kinds of work as engravers, designers, embroiderers in blue, purple and scarlet yarn and fine linen, and weavers—all of them skilled workers and designers.** (35:30-35)

We see from this section of Scripture that God equips his people to do the work he has for them to do. God gifted Bezalel and Oholiab with the wisdom, understanding, knowledge, and skill to make artistic designs. He also gave them the ability to teach. They couldn't do all the work he had for them to do in building the tabernacle and making all the articles for worship. God gifted them with the vision and know-how and the ability to teach so they could teach and oversee the work.

God has work for all of us to do. He's uniquely gifted all of us to do that work. **"From him the whole body, joined and held together by every supporting ligament, grows and builds itself up in love, as each part does its work"** (Ephesians 4:16). If you're not doing your part, then either the work isn't getting done or someone else is doing what God uniquely created them to do plus the work he has for you that you aren't doing. If you've ever been overwhelmed by the amount of work you have to do, you understand it's not a predicament you want to stay in. When we all help out, the work gets done, and it gets done well because we're all doing the things we are meant to do.

If you aren't currently involved with anything at your church and you're able, start with a prayer that God would open your eyes to the things he has prepared for you to do so that you can honor him with your service.

3. The Acts chapter 2 church prayed and broke bread.

They ate together. Hospitality was a big part of the early church.

Everyone has to eat. That makes it a great reason to get together with other believers. It is incredibly encouraging to spend time with others, especially in the busy seasons and the hard seasons. And when you are together, make a point to pray, preferably before and after the meal, when you get together and again before you leave.

A lot of people struggle to pray authentic prayers in front of others. I think we worry that we won't say the right things or it will come out wrong or it will sound silly. I've found just the opposite. When believers get together and say what is on their hearts, it is a beautiful thing. A prayer before the meal can sound as simple as: *God, we thank you for this time together. Thank you for Christian friends and this amazing food. Bless our meal and the conversations we have. In Jesus' name. Amen.*

After spending time together, we usually have a much

better idea of what is going on in the other people's lives. If a couple mentions one of their children is struggling in school, that's something to pray about. If there's tension at work or seasonal depression or a health issue, bring it to the Lord before you end your time together. Again, it doesn't have to be eloquent, just sincere: *Lord, be with Johnny. Help him apply himself and engage in his school subjects. If there's something more going on, make it obvious to his parents. Motivate him to do his best. Amen.*

Hospitality is a spiritual gift. Some people are naturally better at it than others. Some people have a knack for making their houses look cozy and welcoming. Others don't. Here's what I've learned as someone who doesn't bode well in home interior. Clean is great. I don't worry about not having the right pictures or rugs or a modern table. I shoot for a clean house where people feel welcome.

That's it.

Sometimes I make homemade food. Sometimes I get elaborate. But a whole lot of times I don't. Meals are pretty simple. Tacos, chicken potpie, lasagna, or anything Steve grills and chocolate chip cookies or a tuxedo cake from Costco for dessert are my hosting staples. I frequently pray when people come over that the food I make is good, because there have been so many times when that hasn't been the case.

Don't worry if you aren't Martha Stewart. Invite people anyway with or without a meal. Pray with them, talk to them, give them a cup of water and your best encouragement or the best takeout food you can afford at the time. God will take care of the rest.

If you are at a phase in life when you can feed a young family or invite over an elderly person or someone new to church, it is a gift. And if you are elderly and have the time, space, and wherewithal to host someone, do it. You will be blessed as much if not more than the other person.

If it's not an option to have someone over, invite them to go to dinner with you. Put it in your budget to take someone to eat twice a month, and mark it as your personal evangelism fund.

Eating together gives you an opportunity to get to know the person, to explore their heart's desires. It gives you an idea of how to pray for them and discover their needs. It also gives you an opportunity to mentor them or form a relationship that one day may allow you to speak to them about Christ.

And maybe because of their season of life, a meal isn't the best option. Maybe coffee one-on-one is a better option. When my kids were little, I used to meet friends once a month or so for coffee. I cherished the undisturbed time with other moms.

Find time in your schedule somewhere to connect with others. It's one thing that at the end of your life you'll be so thankful you did.

Dip a toe in:

1. If you've never been part of a Bible study, what kind of Bible study would you prefer (small group, large, male/female, in-home)? Why? Is one offered at your church?

2. Do you know your spiritual gifts?

3. Read Romans 12:6–8. Are you gifted in any of those ways?

4. If you've never taken a spiritual gift assessment, take a free one by scanning this code:

5. If you could volunteer at one place, where would it be?

Chapter 7

Smile!

The very first man I took care of as a private elderly companion was a retired pastor who had Alzheimer's. By the time I started working with him, he was confined to a wheelchair and had lost his ability to speak.

I was told that before he was confined to the wheelchair, he was quite the walker. When it became clear that he wasn't able to live on his own, he moved into his daughter's apartment. He walked the halls and wandered often through the subway connecting the apartment building to buildings downtown.

No doubt, this new life in a wheelchair unable to communicate was not his preference. I'm assuming it wouldn't be yours either.

But to say this man didn't communicate would be inaccurate. The way he communicated more often than not was by smiling. When the workers brought his meals, he smiled. When I showed up for work, he smiled. When I squeezed his hand or put my hand on his shoulder, he smiled. When other people came to the table to eat, he smiled. When the nursing assistants came in to help with his care, he smiled.

It makes perfect sense to be known for smiling if and when you are living your best life. If you have a job that doesn't totally stink, a happy family, you are relatively healthy, and you have a place to call home, of course you would smile. And yet, so few of us do.

Day after day, even when we have a more than adequate place to live, have clean drinking water, more food than we can eat in a week, are relatively healthy, have freedoms many people in the world can't imagine, we mope and complain. In fact, if you listen for it, you start to notice how prevalent complaining is.

I already mentioned I went to Vietnam during college. One of several things that rocked my world is how happy everyone seemed. Most people couldn't afford cars. It was a Communist country, so they were not afforded half of the rights we have. Our tour guide's house was smaller than my parents' garage. Many people lived in huts. Family homes often had multiple generations under the same roof. Their diet was simple. Their life was simple. And they smiled. Everywhere we went people were smiling, and because their dental care was nonexistent, they often had toothless grins. It made no sense to me.

The day after returning to America, my now husband and I went to a mall to have lunch and walk around. Seeing so much stuff in all the stores made me physically sick. Steve used to say my trip to Vietnam was one of the best things that I did prior to marriage. When we got married a year to the day after I returned to America, we moved into a house that was a fixer-upper, and even though we didn't have any furniture when we first moved in—not a bed, couch, or living room chair—I was content. I had seen people with far, far less.

You don't have to leave America to recognize that consumerism does not make us happy, but it's a whole lot easier to recognize if you do. Companies have mastered the art of advertising in such a way to push us to covet and live greedy lives. For some reason we are slow to realize all that stuff doesn't make us happier.

If asked, I doubt most of us would consider ourselves greedy. But consider the definition of greed: "an intense and selfish desire for something, especially wealth or power." Again, I think most of us would say, "Phew, I don't want wealth or power, so I'm good."

However, when we live in such a way that much of our income is consumed by our desires; when we'd rather get our nails done, buy a coffee, and have the latest gadget than give to the work of God's kingdom or help others—then our intentions are selfish, lacking consideration for others, concerned chiefly with our own profit or pleasure.

That stings a little, doesn't it?

Only because it hurts to realize we've fallen for the lies of empty promises. We live in a world that tells us more is better. All of us have to determine our standard of living and our capacity to give. Maybe you give what some would consider a large amount of money. If that amount is a drop in the bucket to you, even though it is a large amount, you may still be living a mostly selfish existence.

One day Jesus watched as people made their temple offerings, and he wasn't impressed by the rich people who put in large amounts of money. He was impressed by the poor widow who gave two coins. Why? He told his disciples: **"Truly I tell you, this poor widow has put more into the treasury than all the others. They all gave out of their wealth; but she, out of her poverty, put in everything—all she had to live on"** (Mark 12:43,44).

That is not to say that God demands we give everything we have. It is cautioning us to measure whether or not we've fallen into selfishness and greed, not by the amount that we give but by our capacity to give.

You might wonder what this has to do with smiling. Studies suggest that those who give are healthier and happier than those who don't.[7] Our constant desire for more backfires when it keeps us from being generous.

In fact, we get it wrong all the time. We assume if we get the stuff, then we'll smile, be happy, and have the life we've always wanted. But just like being selfish, the opposite is true.

Joy vs. happiness

The apostle Paul knew that joy isn't dependent on circumstances. Joy is a fruit of the Spirit, a by-product of knowing who you are in Christ and that your identity as a child of God makes you an heir of everlasting life. That's why he was able to write his joy-filled letter to the Philippians while he was imprisoned in Rome. It's why we are happy for a time, short-lived though it is, after getting something but have no more joy than before.

Let me explain. Happiness is a feeling. I can be very happy doing something I shouldn't do. Eating ice cream for breakfast might make me happy. That happiness doesn't last though. Eventually the sugar high becomes a sugar low, and I'm left without energy and a bunch of calories to burn off.

Buying new stuff can make me happy, but that same happiness I feel at the time I buy the new stuff could throw the Swenson budget out the door. The happiness lasts only until the credit card bills arrive, and then my happiness is replaced with dread.

I could be entertaining and not only happy myself but make others happy too if I made a habit of getting drunk. But that happiness is transient. Once the buzz fades, so does the feeling of being happy. Now I'm filled with regret, I feel sluggish, and I need more alcohol to get happy again.

Joy, however, isn't a feeling. It's the sense that all is well, whether or not things are going the way we hoped they would and whether or not we understand what's happening at all. In Matthew chapter 28, Matthew recounts what occurred on Easter morning. The women went to the tomb to finish the anointing of Jesus' body, but the tomb was empty. The women didn't see Jesus, but they saw an angel who told them to go tell the disciples that Jesus had risen from the dead.

We don't consider often enough the emotional roller coaster these women were on. They had watched their friend and Savior die a brutal death just days prior. They were mourning and bewildered and going through the motions when their world was shaken again. Jesus was gone. What did it mean that he'd risen?

Next we read, **"So the women hurried away from the tomb, afraid yet filled with joy, and ran to tell his disciples"** (Matthew 28:8). They were afraid, but they were also filled with joy. Those are two drastically different emotions.

They were the same two emotions the shepherds felt the first Christmas night. When the angels appeared in the field over Bethlehem, the shepherds were terrified. But when the angels returned to heaven, the shepherds hurried off to find the baby, and once they had seen him, they joyfully told everyone about him.

Author Randy Alcorn writes: "In Christ's day, shepherds stood on the bottom rung of the Palestinian social ladder. They shared the same unenviable status as tax collectors and dung sweepers. Only Luke mentions them."[8]

Luke 2:20 says, **"The shepherds returned, glorifying and praising God for all the things they had heard and seen, which were just as they had been told."** Nothing had changed in their social status that night. They were the same shepherds who people looked down on. Nothing had changed for them financially either. But they were filled with joy because everything changed for them spiritually. The Messiah had come. Their Father in heaven acted on their behalf. And even more amazingly, he made sure *they* knew about it.

That is joy. Joy is the delight we feel knowing our status in heaven no matter what our status is on earth. It is recognizing that a whole lot doesn't matter. We could be in the best place we've ever been or the worst, the healthiest or the sickest, the richest or poorest, lonely, surrounded by friends, or anywhere in between. Nothing can take away joy because it isn't dependent on anything we do or have.

And here's the thing: If your friends are all about happiness, as a lot of friends are, they may or may not be lifelong friends. If you are drinking buddies, then as long as the drinks keep coming, it's a good time. But as soon as one or the other of you has to cut back, the good time comes to a stop. The friends you shop with, vacation with, play golf with, eat out with last as long as your happiness lasts.

Joy is different. Relationships based on the joy of knowing the Lord and trusting his plan for your lives are rooted in Christ. That foundation is not easily shaken.

Those women who followed Jesus and cared for his needs, who experienced fear and joy that first Easter morning, would never be the same. The shepherds too witnessed and experienced something that would bind them for life.

Meet another brother or sister in Christ, a believer who walks with God, reads his Word, and takes his commands seriously and you will know the joy of Christian fellowship almost instantaneously.

Many years ago, I was at a local Christian bookstore doing a book signing. A young man walked in and asked about my book. It was a Bible study for moms, so clearly he wasn't the intended audience, but we had a nice conversation about ministry, goals, etc. When he left, he said to me: "Hey, nice meeting you. See you when we get home."

I've never forgotten that. It felt genuine in all the right ways at the time. It was a reminder that God's people are everywhere and that when we meet them, so often there is a bond that's unexplainable.

The joy of the Lord is like glitter. It spreads inexplicably. Even when things are not great, being together with God's people makes it worthwhile. We energize and motivate each other, pray and encourage each other. We help each other remember that our earthly existence is transitory but a day is coming when we will be home with the Lord forever.

Ideally, it's noticeable to believers and unbelievers alike. Believers have a way of spurring one another on, and unbelievers notice you don't get dragged down by circumstances and give in to despair or grumbling.

Smile through it all

I've seen that pastor I took care of change the mood of a room more than once with his smile. The housekeeper might come in to clean his room in a terrible mood because nothing was going right. But he smiled. Then she smiled. Then we were all smiling. Did it change the whole day? Maybe not. But it conveyed the message that if he could smile in his condition, maybe the things she was fretting about weren't worth the emotional energy she was giving them.

Entrepreneur Alex Hormozi, who from what I've seen doesn't appear to have a religious affiliation says, "If you can be in a bad mood for no reason, you might as well be in a good mood for no reason." The apostle Paul said as much when he proclaimed, **"Rejoice in the Lord always. I will say it again: Rejoice!"** (Philippians 4:4). Remember, he wrote that from prison.

Expect things to go wrong. We live in a sinful world where they will. Some days you won't feel great. The car will break. The kids will misbehave. You'll get in an argument with your spouse. But it doesn't have to result in a bad day. All those things are reasons to pray and reasons to give thanks. If you have a spouse, children, and a car, you have many reasons to give thanks, even when they aren't behaving the way you hoped. Some days will go better than others. But you have a God to turn to. And he isn't a wimpy God. He is the Almighty God, Creator of the universe.

Be a friend who reminds others how good it feels to give to people who are in need and to invest in things that have eternal returns.

And smile. That pastor who I took care of, his smile preached a sermon as meaningful as any he ever preached from the pulpit. His smile said, *"God is on the throne. God's will is good. I am the Lord's servant; may it be to me whatever he wills. My times are in his hands. I am content."*

That can encourage all of us to do the same and to be open to the relationships around us, whatever they may be.

If you are lonely, consider your demeanor. Maybe you

aren't a jokester or an extrovert. Do you invite conversation? Do you smile? While working at the nursing home, I always made a point of smiling. I tried to be a cheery reminder that God had given the resident and me another day.

A smile costs nothing. If you really are at a stage in life when giving financially is tough, give from your wealth of affection. Be on the lookout for recipients. Smile, and when appropriate, give people a hug. Hug your grown children; hug your mom and dad. If there's a woman at church whose grown children don't live nearby, hug her and tell her it's a hug from her kids. And don't leave those sour-faced old men out. They may look like they are going to bite your head off, but they often melt when they get affection.

These are the keys to fulfilling relationships. Genuine concern for your fellow man manifested in heartfelt actions make for meaningful connection. That happens when you can look past your struggles and let the joy of the Lord pour out of you.

And let me tell you, if you are able to smile and laugh your way through even the hardest of times, you will be an absolute joy to be around. While on a European cruise, I met a couple on the sundeck. They were easy to talk to, and Steve and I enjoyed a brief conversation with them. The next night I went on the deck to walk and saw the woman, so we strolled together. When I tell you laughter came easy for this couple, it is an understatement. Wherever they were on the ship or on the bus, it was not unusual to hear them laughing.

Clearly their lives were pretty easy, right? Not by a long shot. She was experiencing health issues. He had job struggles. They had aging parents and the responsibilities that went along with it.

There was another man on the cruise whom I had a chance to get to know briefly. We shared the same sense of humor, so he often said something that made me laugh or vice versa. The last night we were all together was not particularly happy. All of us were saying goodbye, knowing we might not see each other again, and if we did, the opportunities would be few and far between. I had already started crying when I went to say goodbye to this man and his wife. And you know what we did? We started laughing. His laugh made me laugh, and we laughed some more.

The hard, the horrid, the sad times will come. Some days we won't be able to laugh. But we can still smile, letting the world know that we have the joy of the Lord in our hearts, that he is good and has everything under control.

Dip a toe in:

1. What is the biggest factor that keeps you from feeling joy (delight connected to a sense of well-being)?

2. Is whatever you named above something in your control to change?

3. Have you prayed for God to instill joy in your life?

4. What have you been waiting for, thinking it will fill you with joy?

5. If God is the source of joy, what will you do to get more God in your life?

Chapter 8

You Already Belong

At the beginning of 1 Peter chapter 2, the apostle Peter explains that Jesus was rejected by some. But to those of us who believe, he became the most important thing: the Cornerstone, the One on whom the foundation of our faith is built. Peter goes on to say that some people stumble over this information, but not believers. This is how Peter describes those who believe in Jesus: **"You are a chosen people, a royal priesthood, a holy nation, God's special possession, that you may declare the praises of him who called you out of darkness into his wonderful light"** (verse 9).

Those who believe in Jesus are chosen, royal, holy, God's special possessions. Those are not words to move over quickly. Let's break them down.

Chosen

The word *chosen* means "being selected as the best or most appropriate." The night Jesus was arrested and subsequently crucified, John records Jesus saying, **"You did not choose me, but I chose you"** (15:16).

Being in God's family is no small thing. It's not

something we can earn. We have nothing to attract God to us. Members of God's family to go into God's presence any day, any time through prayer and reading the Bible. We have access to the Holy Spirit who comforts, guides, directs, and strengthens us. When we are at a loss for words, he swoops in on our behalf to tell the Father what we need. And as children of God, we are heirs to an eternal home with God forever. If that doesn't make you smile, nothing will.

Royal

Royal means "to share the status of a king or queen." Thanks to Jesus' sacrifice, believers are not peasants in God's kingdom. In Romans 8:17, the apostle Paul calls believers coheirs with Christ. Most leaders are thrilled to show their dominance over those who serve them. But not Jesus.

> **"You know that the rulers of the Gentiles lord it over them, and their high officials exercise authority over them. Not so with you. Instead, whoever wants to become great among you must be your servant, and whoever wants to be first must be your slave—just as the Son of Man did not come to be served, but to serve, and to give his life as a ransom for many."** (Matthew 20:25-29)

Christ took our place so we could reign with him forever in eternity. Grace doesn't make sense. Why would perfect, sinless Jesus serve someone like me? It's undeserved. That's what makes it such a gift.

Holy

Holy means "set apart or dedicated to God." In the Old Testament, many articles in the temple were set apart for use in the temple. We too are set apart. We're not like the people of the world who live for today and whatever pleasures they can get. We live for God's glory, knowing the best is yet to come.

God's special possession

Finally, believers are God's special possessions. We aren't like old socks that get lost in a corner. We are treasured possessions, something to display. God knows who each of us is, where we are, and what is on our hearts. He keeps track of every hair on our heads. Our walls and issues are always before him.

That means even if you don't feel all that special, even if you don't feel you have that many good friends, even if you haven't found your church home or your small group or your best friends yet, you already belong in God's family. And that's an honor and privilege unlike any other.

If you are a member of a church, you also belong to a family of believers much like the Acts chapter 2 church we've been studying throughout this book.

Here's what you need to remember. No family is perfect.

Every family has its issues. Every family is made up of imperfect people who have weaknesses and strengths.

Some fathers are structured and hardcore. Some are whimsical. Some struggle and depend on their wives. Some wives are organized, some are happy-go-lucky, and some nurture to a fault.

Leaders in the church are also gifted differently. One church's pastor is rigid, while the next is laid back. One runs a tight ship; the next has others steering the ship.

That's just to say all families get messy at times. All churches will go through struggles. There will be times when the enemies are outside the church and other times when the enemies are within. In either case, believers will have to rely on God's Word and the strength he provides through prayer.

While it would be Disney-like if every story had a happy ending, the truth is that sometimes things don't go the way you hope. Sometimes boundaries need to be put in place. You'll have to determine what you will or won't do. Other times the boundary will be that you'll need to walk away for the sake of peace. But that doesn't mean that your identity has changed. Even if you walk away from one group of believers, you still belong in God's family. Even if your own family hasn't worked out the way you hoped, you are still loved by God. And sometimes you just need a little break or a separation for a time while God works in your heart and the heart of the other person.

Prior to his conversion, Paul, known as Saul, threw

some Christians in jail and murdered others. Jesus appeared to him and opened his eyes to the fact that by persecuting the church, Saul was persecuting him. Saul repented and became a Christian, but initially everyone was too scared to believe he was a Christian because he had persecuted the church so zealously.

Barnabas was a trusted leader of the early church. He took Saul under his wing and brought him to the apostles. Barnabas also took Saul on his first mission trip. It was on this first missionary journey that Saul started being called Paul, and the leadership role changed.

But then, in Acts 15:36–41, Luke records a disagreement between Paul and Barnabas:

> **Sometime later Paul said to Barnabas, "Let us go back and visit the believers in all the towns where we preached the word of the Lord and see how they are doing." Barnabas wanted to take John, also called Mark, with them, but Paul did not think it wise to take him, because he had deserted them in Pamphylia and had not continued with them in the work. They had such a sharp disagreement that they parted company. Barnabas took Mark and sailed for Cyprus, but Paul chose Silas and left, commended by the believers to the grace of the Lord. He went through Syria and Cilicia, strengthening the churches.**

Clearly both men were godly. Both men had a heart for taking the gospel to the world. And in this predicament, which God deemed necessary to record for all time, the two men couldn't reach an agreement.

That's good for us to keep in mind. They were both still part of the family of believers. But sometimes the answer is to walk away from a situation for a season. It doesn't mean the other person is bad or wrong. It doesn't mean you are either of those things either. It means, at least for a time, you can't agree and to stay and continue fighting would be unproductive.

No church can do everything. Churches and ministries have to set their goals and their courses. They choose who they want in positions of leadership, and much like Paul refusing to go along with John Mark, sometimes the person a church or ministry chooses is not your choice for whatever reason. The apostle Paul tells us in Romans 12:18 that when possible, we should strive to live at peace with everyone. And Luke, who wrote the book of Acts, reminds us that sometimes, for a time, it's not possible to be at peace.

What hope does this ultimately give us? As you read the epistles of Paul, it becomes clear that later in life John Mark became a dear ministry partner to him. The hesitancy he had may have been inexcusable at the time, but John Mark proved himself to be a worthy ministry partner with Barnabas, Peter, and later Paul.

That's good for us to remember. Maybe you're in a difficult season with someone at church. Maybe your family is going through difficult times, or you're split on a course of action for aging parents or any number of issues. The disagreements you are in make you feel alone, not like you belong. This too will pass. Someday the things that cause you to lose sleep right now will be water under the bridge. And some of the very people who let you down once upon a time may end up being wonderful later in life.

That isn't entirely comforting in the moment, especially when feelings are hurt and you had your heart set on a certain course. God sees. He knows. Whatever happens, everyone will be judged by God, and he weighs motives. If your motives are pure and you're acting in accordance to what you deem best at the time, do what you can. If you try and you're outvoted, then you've done your part. God sees that too.

Just remember your opinion is one opinion. Sometimes you don't see or understand the whole picture, and other times, even if you are right, others decide to go a different way.

Notice that when Paul and Barnabas disagreed, neither crawled into bed and pulled the covers over his head. Barnabas went one way, and Paul went another way, continuing to do the work of the Lord. When your family is a mess and no one is listening to you, when your church is struggling and your words are falling on deaf ears, find what you can do and do it with all your heart, asking God to show you if you're wrong and giving you places to do ministry. It is exactly in times like this that Christians go into the world and volunteer at a hospital or an airport or another nonprofit. And their efforts may go further than they ever would have in their family or church building. Just don't curl up in a ball and give up. Satan would love if you did that. As hard as it can be at the time, it's important to remember that you are chosen, royal, holy, and God's special possession. That equips you to do what you do, even if you have to go somewhere else to do it.

Paul also didn't go to every new church and make a case for why he chose Silas and why John Mark was not a good option. That would have undermined the work of the gospel. So, too, when our family or church family is going through issues, find your few friends who you can tell the whole story to, who can walk you through the mess and help you see what you might not be able to see, and then let God sort it out. We don't have to put it all on social media or make our case with everyone who will listen. God saw and heard everything that happened, and he knows better than anyone what everyone was thinking. Our prayers can be for God to work all things for good and to work in mighty ways, even if he works in ways we don't understand.

Be open to resolution. Maybe for a time or a season you have to walk away. That doesn't mean that relationship won't be mended somewhere down the line. It means for a season and for the sake of everyone involved you remove yourself from the situation. Forgive whatever has hurt you. Work through whatever you need to be healed from. And if it is safe and wise, be open to a relationship down the line, knowing God is in the business of restoration.

The older I get, the more I realize I'm not always right.

Even if I have a good idea, it may not mean that it's the right thing to do at the time. Even if it would be the right thing to do at the time and would make a dramatic difference in a situation, if a family or church doesn't have the money, manpower, or ambition to do it, it isn't feasible at the time.

In a family and in the church, God asks us to submit to the leaders that were established. If your aging parents made one child their medical power of attorney, they did so for a reason, entrusting their medical decisions to that child. When that child makes a decision based on what he or she sees at the time and his or her knowledge of care, the other children can give their opinion but ultimately need to submit. When church leadership makes a decision based on what they know of manpower, budget, etc., the rest of us submit.

If it's the wrong decision, God will take care of it. He won't hold it against you. Don't fret if things don't go your way. Don't fret when relationships are messy or when for a time you have to walk away or submit and go a direction you didn't want to go. God sees everything and will reward you for trusting him. The body of believers is far from perfect, and neither are we. As we sojourn through our days, we look to God and wise people around us for guidance when decisions need to be made and trust him for the strength to endure wherever those decisions or the decisions of others take us.

Perhaps if there's one last lesson, it is this: to be open to the new people God puts in your life as he works things out. You belong in God's family, but so do a whole lot of others.

And incredible blessing can happen when you're open to new relationships.

When Paul disagreed with Barnabas, he took Silas. The disagreement made room for another person to be involved and two groups to go out instead of just one.

Three friends became crucial ministry partners to me just in the last few years. In 2022 we decided to be deliberate about our relationship and marked off a weekend to rent a house and get together for the purpose of writing, talking through our ministry ideas, praying, recording podcasts, and reading the Bible together. The following year we met again. Amazing blessings came out of our time together.

The Lord in his wisdom called one of these sisters in Christ home in 2024. Since then, the other two women and I have been at several events. We always make a point to spend time together, but not always exclusively. One by one each of us will be called home. And though the Lord has blessed us with a beautiful relationship, God puts other people in our lives too.

Note this from Acts 2:47: **"And the Lord added to their number daily those who were being saved."**

God added. That means we need to be open to new relationships, new people joining our churches and family and small groups and all the things. And that can be hard. Dynamics will change, and at times we'll experience the pain of that growth. We'll need to remember that just because things were one way before, new people mean new ideas and new ideas are not necessarily bad. We're never too old to make new friends, and I hope I never feel like I have enough friends. And that means being open to new relationships rather than closed off and being willing to put in the effort to meet new people.

Steve and I have been in the same small group for the 20 years the group has met. During that time, we've started other small groups that eventually fizzled. Have we quit forming small groups? I hope not.

I hope I continue to meet new people and form new friendships and new ministry partners. I hope I never get to the point of thinking I have enough people in my life. I would miss out if I do.

When you read the Bible, you notice God is the God of abundance. He never once answered a prayer by saying he was all out of power or supplies or energy.

When the people of Israel needed water in the desert, God gave them water. When they needed food, God gave them food. When they were stuck with a sea in front of them and Egypt's chariots behind them, God opened the sea. He chided Moses for doubting he could give meat to the whole company of Israelites. **"Now you will see whether or not what I say will come true for you,"** he told him (Numbers 11:23).

In fact, account after account after account in the Bible reminds us over and over and over again that nothing is impossible with God. His love doesn't run out. His power doesn't have a limit. He doesn't exclude people who don't seem quite right. Jesus called tax collectors, prostitutes, those who had been demon possessed, and a woman who had been married five times and was living with someone she wasn't married to.

That's not to say you shouldn't be discerning. Not every person your son or daughter dates is meant to be part of your family. And not every person who comes to your church has good intentions. So when you're not quite sure if you should include that person, pray about it, talk to a trusted friend, and maybe for a time give it a try. God knows their heart and their motives, and in time it will become clear.

In the meantime, be friendly and welcoming. Be generous with your invitations and relish the people God puts in your life.

Dip a toe in:

1. What is the biggest advantage of being part of the great company of all believers of all time?

2. Who would you love to get to know if given the chance?

3. Is there anyone in your life like that person?

4. Name two to five people in your life whom you would invite to church or to a Bible study or whom you've always wanted to invite to coffee.

5. Make a plan: Pray about it, choose one name, and invite them.

Conclusion

I've learned many things in the last five or six years, not the least of which is that if there's something I don't like about my life, a lot of times I have the power to change it. Not always. A disease may take things from you or me that we can't get back. But a lot of times, we have more freedom than we imagine.

Often the real issue is a lack of self-awareness and (this is a big *and*) not paying attention to what the real issues are and/or refusing to try another way.

Possibly the most important thing I've learned is not to be afraid. Try something. If it doesn't work, try something else. The people who are the most joy filled are not more special than you. They've just learned to pivot. If something isn't working, they do something else.

That's what the apostle Paul did. He went somewhere, and if he was kicked out, he went somewhere else. He was shipwrecked, beaten, imprisoned. Wherever he went he found people. Not all of them liked him. Some of them hated him. That didn't stop him.

Don't be afraid to fail. So much learning comes from failing. So much winning comes from trying. If most of your relationships have been failures, then learn from the experiences and move on. The key is to learn.

Keep your goals small. You don't need 50 friends. You need a handful of really amazing people who know you well and can encourage you and pray you through. It is helpful to be the kind of person whom your neighbors can approach, anyone at church can ask a question of, or someone people don't run away from. It would be even better to be a spark, to be the kind of person who notices the people not everyone does, who builds people up, strengthens the weak, and reminds people of the hope they have in Jesus.

It only takes a spark to light a fire. You can be the spark in your neighborhood, your church, your office, your nursing home. You can be the one who radiates joy and points people to a loving God who loves relationship.

If your wick is smoldering, God won't snuff it out. Pray God helps you find the people who can fan your flame. And don't be afraid to reach out. Ask someone to coffee or for a walk. The worst they can say is no.

If I don't see you before, see you when we get home.

Questions for Self-Reflection

This exercise is not meant to make you feel guilty. Instead, it's meant to help you grow as you seek deeper relationships, knowing you are in need of a Savior but holding on to the forgiveness Jesus won for you. Go forward in God's grace.

Take a look at your normal day-to-day routine. What do you do when you get up?

Whom do you talk to and/or listen to and for how long?

If you are still working, examine your workday. How often do you engage with coworkers?

How would your coworkers describe your attitude?

If you aren't working or work from home, how often do you interact with other people? Do you initiate conversations, texts, opportunities to get together?

Would you say you are generally easygoing, friendly, fun loving, and easy to talk to, or might others find you critical, high stress, intolerable?

Do others generally seem excited to see you, or do they tend to feel out your mood?

Is it more likely that you are the one encouraging others, or if you're honest, are you the person who always has something to complain about, always has another issue, always needs someone to walk you away from the edge?

Are you rigid and controlling, easily pointing out what others are doing that doesn't measure up?

Are you judgmental about people who don't have their lives in order?

Are you embarrassed by the way you look, the way your house looks, the state of your yard, the way you respond, or embarrassed of your spouse?

Do you tend to dominate conversations, or do you ask people about their lives, what they've been up to, how they are feeling?

What are the things you are avoiding?

When was the last time you shared with someone how they can pray for you?

Are you a divider or a unifier? If you look at the past five years, have you worked to encourage and bring people together or are your attitude and actions more likely to cause division?

Can you keep a secret?

Notes

1. *Concordia Self-Study Bible* (Grand Rapids, MI: Zondervan Publishing House, 1984), 1453.

2. *Concordia Self-Study Bible*, 1619.

3. *Concordia Self-Study Bible*, 1609.

4. PLOS, "Satisfying friendships could be key for young, single adults' happiness," ScienceDaily, http://www.sciencedaily.com/releases/2024/10/241002154120.htm (accessed October 13, 2025).

5. "The Role of Silence in Conversation," *Campfire*, May 16, 2022, https://www.getcampfire.com/blog/the-role-of-silence-in-conversation#:~:text=It%20builds%20better%20relationships,filter%20and%20condense%20their%20ideas.

6. Emily Stone, "Sitting Near a High-Performer Can Make You Better at Your Job," *KelloggInsight*, May 8, 2017, https://insight.kellogg.northwestern.edu/article/sitting-near-a-high-performer-can-make-you-better-at-your-job.

7. Laura Phillips, "6 Surprising Benefits of Being a Generous Person," Compassion, February 19, 2024, https://www.compassion.ca/blog/6-surprising-benefits-of-being-a-generous-person/#:~:text=2.,recorded%20more%20negativity%20and%20stress.

8. Randy Alcorn, "Shepherd Status," *Eternal Perspectives*, Winter 2009, https://www.epm.org/static/uploads/pdf_newsletters/09winter.pdf.

About the Author

Amber Albee Swenson has authored several books and is a regular blogger and podcaster for Time of Grace. Mostly she's amazed at God's goodness, awed by his wisdom and desire to grow her, and continually stretched by his calling in her life. For more details about her ministry, go to her website: amberalbeeswenson.com. Listen to Amber's podcast, *Little Things*, on YouTube, Spotify, Apple Podcasts, and many other podcasting platforms.

Other books by Amber

The Key to Confidence:
Where to Go When You Feel You're Not Enough

You Can Trust God When Life Hurts

Soul Care:
Nurturing Your Spiritual Wellness

Find these books and more on Amazon.

About Time of Grace

The mission of Time of Grace is to point people to what matters most: Jesus. Using a variety of media (television, radio, podcasts, print publications, and digital), Time of Grace teaches tough topics in an approachable and relatable way, accessible in multiple languages, making the Bible clear and understandable for those who need encouragement in their walks of faith and for those who don't yet know Jesus at all.

To discover more, please visit timeofgrace.org or scan this code:

Help share God's message of grace!

Every gift you give helps Time of Grace reach people around the world with the good news of Jesus. Your generosity and prayer support take the gospel of grace to others through our ministry outreach and help them experience a satisfied life as they see God all around them.

Give today at timeofgrace.org/give,
by calling 800.661.3311,
or by scanning the code below.

Thank you!